CHRISTIAN
liberty

Also by Rex M. Rogers

Seducing America: Is Gambling a Good Bet?

CHRISTIAN
liberty

LIVING *for* GOD
IN A
CHANGING CULTURE

REX M.
ROGERS

Baker Books

A Division of Baker Book House Co
Grand Rapids, Michigan 49516

Published by Baker Books
a division of Baker Book House Company
P.O. Box 6287, Grand Rapids, MI 49516-6287
www.bakerbooks.com

Printed in the United States of America

Library of Congress Cataloging-in-Publication Data is on file at the Library of Congress, Washington, D. C.

ISBN 0-8010-6460-0

To my wife, Sarah Lee Stone Rogers,

whose love remains constant amidst change and
who enjoys with me both life and liberty

CONTENTS

ACKNOWLEDGMENTS

This book was first conceived as a project for publication nineteen years ago. Then my idea was to connect a discussion of social change with the arrival of the "dreaded year" George Orwell made famous in his book *1984*. It might have worked, but then life happened. Changes—spiritual, personal, professional, and global—too numerous to mention followed one after the other in a trainload of experiences that delayed but, in the providence of God, eventually contributed to the project. I've wanted to write this book for a long time, but I pray the slow percolation has made it a better blend.

I am greatly indebted to many people for helping me form the ideas in this book. Chief among those people is my wife, Sarah. After our wedding day those many years ago, we at last found ourselves in the ironic and beautiful state of matrimony—alone together, having to make our own decisions. Both of us had been blessed with Christian parents who provided us a strong and loving introduction to Christian faith and practice. That upbringing, together with a Christian higher education, gave Sarah and me a start in adult decision making that I wish for everyone.

Our children, Elizabeth, Eric, Andrew, and Adam, added greatly to our lives and required that we think through *why we believe what we believe* and what was important to instill in them. We found teaching children to be a learning experience.

Sarah's commitment to Christ and to the principles of biblical Christianity has never wavered. Together we came to understand that liberty is most enjoyed in obedience to God's Word. While this book contains *my* views, it would not exist without *our* experience.

To Doug and Irene DeLand and Bob and Carol Opperman we owe a debt. They have been our friends since early adulthood, and we have spent many hours discussing how Christians apply (or biblically should apply) their faith to lifestyle issues in a changing world, and more specifically in Christian schools, churches, and families. Those long evening talks helped hone many of the thoughts found in this book.

Nearly countless discussions with faculty, staff, trustees, and students at Cornerstone University and previous institutions where I have served also have provided me with an opportunity to practice spiritual discernment. Learning how to apply the Christian worldview to life and culture and then teaching students how to do the same are central to the mission of the truly Christian university experience. I learned with everyone else.

Two people deserve special credit because, independently and consistently, they would not let the idea for this book die—Len Galloway and Randy Bronkema. Len is the husband of a now retired but longtime and beloved faculty member of Cornerstone University, Dr. Orpha Galloway. In our relationship over more than ten years, every time I saw the man—and I do mean *every* time—he asked me about the status of this book. Then he'd encourage, beg, cajole, and "threaten" me to get it completed because he so deeply believes the Christian community is being needlessly torn apart by disagreements in the culture wars. Len, your confidence and dogged determination were something I needed. Thank you.

Randy Bronkema works with me as the university's chief advancement officer. Randy's gift and his key word is *passion*. He knows that leaders really aren't worth much unless they believe in something. Randy knew my convictions on the subject of this book. Even more, he passionately believes that each person needs to contribute, to make a mark. I benefited greatly from Randy's spiritual conscience and intensity and the direct encouragement he has given me to lead for the cause of Christ. I hope some of Randy's passion reaches the readers of this text.

David J. Ayers, Richard Daniel Burke, Ron Burwell, Tony Carnes, D. Bruce Lockerbie, James G. McGoldrick, Udo W. Middelmann, David O. Moberg, Herbert Schlossberg, and Gary Scott Smith provided comments on the parts of this text dealing with social change. Their critique was given years before the remainder of the text was developed, but their insights lost nothing in the passage of time.

Cornerstone professors Mark Blocher, Gary Meadors, Andy Smith, and Mike Wittmer read parts of the text, supplying insightful criticism. And then there were more long discussions with Cornerstone staff and faculty Matt Bonzo, Tim Cosby, Tim Detwiler, Tom Emigh, Bob Fortosis, Brian Jackson, Rick Newberry, Chuck Swanson, and John Verberkmoes. I benefited from their knowledge of the Word of God, their wisdom, and their experience in living and working within the Christian community.

Several individuals gave me the benefit of their counsel as this book was prepared for publication: Charles Alber, Robert C. Andringa, Alvin O. Austin, Jennie Afman Dimkoff, David S. Dockery, Stan Gaede, Nick Kroeze, Al Meredith, and Gary Scott Smith. Each person shared his or her insights on the value and potential audience of this work and for this I am grateful.

First Maxine Nelson and then later Marsha Ledbetter, my executive assistants at Cornerstone University, managed the work of the president's office and kept me on track in that responsibility as I developed the text. They also handled with professionalism and grace periodic online searches and printing responsibilities.

I am also grateful to my editor, Mary Suggs, for her expertise in writing and insightful advice. Her work made this a better book.

All of these individuals have helped to build my life and therefore have influenced the construction of this book. None is responsible for the judgments or errors that may be found within.

The book of James proclaims, "Faith without works is dead." I trust that this work is an apt expression of a living faith.

Introduction

CHRISTIAN THEMES IN CHANGING TIMES

As you sent me into the world, I have sent them into the world.

John 17:18

The story is told of an old farmer who loved to fish and who served as a deacon in his local church. When the young pastor convened deacons' meetings, the old farmer would sit for long periods saying nothing. He'd listen to the interminable discussions about seemingly weighty but rather arcane matters and eventually, when asked his opinion, would simply say, "Small fish." In response to very few issues, the farmer would say, "Big fish." After several weeks of this behavior, the young pastor finally worked up the courage to ask the old gentleman what his comments meant. The old farmer said, "Son, when I catch a fish that's too small, I throw it back. I only get excited and spend my time on the big fish."

The moral of the story is, of course, that Christians are adept at wasting hours on "small-fish" issues. We major on the minors and, as a result, sometimes miss the majors. We need to focus our attention and our spiritual energy on "big-fish" issues. Anything less than this makes us ineffective "fishers of men."

Big-Fish and Small-Fish Social Change

This book is about Christians struggling with social change. It's not about biblical Christianity struggling with social change, because it's not God who struggles; he knows what he's doing. It's Christians who struggle. We (and I'll keep saying "we," for I'm a Christian too) Christians don't handle social change very well.

On one level Christians, along with everyone else, are buffeted by rapid and far-reaching social change. However you want to look at it, the culture in which we live is experiencing enormous and comprehensive social change. We're witnessing the declining influence of one culture and its underlying values, what's been called *Modernity,* and the growing influence of another culture and its underlying values, something we call *Postmodernity.*

If you could think of Modernity as a dinner party, religion, including biblical Christianity, would be the uninvited guest. Religion was sent away from the cultural table, so to speak, by Modernity. Human reason took its place at the head of Modernity's table, with science seated on one side and technology seated on the other. Some of the other guests included humanism and a process called secularization that de-emphasizes all religions.

Postmodernity's guest list is different. Postmodernity tolerates religion, including biblical Christianity, at the table once again. But biblical Christianity is invited back to the table under Postmodernity's own terms and along with innumerable other philosophy or worldview guests, like spiritualism and New Age thought. Postmodernity doesn't seem to put any one worldview at the head of the table. In fact it appears that Postmodernity suggests there is no head of the table. No philosophy is favored at all, except possibly moral relativism—the idea that truth or absolutes of right and wrong do not exist.

Far-reaching, life-influencing social change of this magnitude, particularly its moral relativism, is producing a culture crisis in the United States and in other so-called developed countries of the world. It is the "big fish" of our day. "Crisis" sounds a bit over the top, and if we were simply talking about a new toy or tool, it would be. But we're not talking about new things; we're talking about changes in basic values, the way we think about the world. This big fish is showing up in education, religion, business, entertainment, medicine, politics, and more.

Some Christians aren't sure what to make of this culture crisis. Many Christians are confused by it, and most haven't applied their Christian faith to these current cultural issues.

On another level a lot of Christians are distracted by social change in their churches or, more broadly, the Christian community. Christians are confused about which church practices or methods (like music or church service format) and which personal lifestyle choices (like fads and fashions or entertainment) they should embrace or reject. Since we're not sure what to do, most of us retreat to the false security of rules and traditions. We develop codes of behavior God never commanded, ones that limit more than liberate our Christian impact on the world. Passions are running so high in these debates that Christians have found themselves in a multi-issue, continuous culture war within the church.

My experience in Christian higher education has been one long culture war. The Christian community is incredibly sensitive to cultural concerns. For example, many are quick to conclude that an entire school is un-Christian because of the music played before a basketball game, and they're all too willing to act as judge, jury, and executioner. In the name of Christian character, Christians write amazingly torrid, even nasty letters of criticism before checking their facts. And they send copies of such letters to board members, area pastors, and anyone else they think may respond to their power play.

Christians accuse the school of improper conduct because they see one student with long hair or unnaturally colored hair or moussed hair. In this culture war scenario, if the school does not confiscate students' questionable music CDs, then the school must be condoning the worst of contemporary music. If students are taught spiritual discernment as opposed to a rules-based approach to student spiritual formation, then the school is "going liberal." If a faculty member doesn't wear a tie, he and the school must surely be departing from the faith. If a student praise band is used in chapel services, featuring guitars and drums rather than piano and organ, then the school is pandering to contemporary whims. If a faculty member reads the Harry Potter books and liked the first film, then clearly no one at that school knows anything about the Christian faith, and so it goes, on and on and on.

Meanwhile, none of these generally well-meaning Christians examines the school's confession of faith. No one asks to review the school's mission statement or Christian philosophy of education. Very few Christian critics ever try to discover what the school means when we discuss Christian worldview and how it applies to all of life. The critics, our own version of Nehemiah's Sanballat, Tobiah, and Geshem, demonstrate they are better at just being critical than at critical analysis of the cultural issues at hand.

One of the reasons Christians are struggling with these culture wars is that their theological understanding is either underdeveloped or ambiguous. Another is that many Christians equate their Christian faith with given cultural practices; then they judge others' spirituality on that basis. Either way, the result is the same—a lot of heat with very little light, impeded evangelism, and limited impact on our culture.

These issues are the small fish. I don't mean any disrespect for the people who fight these battles, for many of them are dedicated Christian people trying to do what they think God wants them to do. I do mean that these small-fish battles are not as important as the big-fish social changes, some of which stem from worldviews antithetical to biblical Christianity. And fighting these small-fish issues is not as important as our God-given responsibility to influence our neighbors and our neighborhood culture for Christ.

The postmodern culture crisis in which we find ourselves demands more of us than warm, fuzzy feelings or pop-Christian sentimentalities. It demands more of us than a superficial knowledge of the Bible. Expressing our Christian faith is important, but we'll need to do it in more meaningful ways than the correct but simplistic "Praise Jesus!" of many contemporary choruses or the "Hey Taliban, Get Saved" slogans on T-shirts. We will not be able to proclaim the truth of the Christian faith in the midst of this culture crisis if we believe that biblical Christianity is nice but just for our private lives. Christians who march in the Lord's army in this age must learn to think with a Christian worldview that speaks to all of life.

LOVING THE LORD WITH ALL OUR MINDS

Sometimes we forget that God gave us a brain as well as a heart. He expects us to use them both. God never told us, "Check your brains at the door of the church." Yet "comprehensive and coherent

Christian thinking has never been a major part of religious life in America."[1] Christians are not generally known for their well-conceived interpretations of life and culture, so much so that Harry Blamires said, "There is no longer a Christian mind."[2] He was discouraged and he meant that we don't operate with a distinctively Christian philosophy of life.

A less friendly observer, Bertrand Russell, put an ironic twist on the problem, once saying, "Most Christians would rather die than think. In fact, they do."[3] Unfortunately, his comment rings disturbingly true. Christians have frequently been content to "turn off the mind and toe the line."[4]

But Jesus said, "Love the Lord your God with all your heart and with all your soul and with all your mind and with all your strength" (Mark 12:30; see also Matt. 22:37). Our minds are important to God. He created both faith and reason. Our sovereign God is truth, and biblical Christianity is a logical faith. Others may escape from reason but not Christians. Biblical revelation is a testimony to Christians that not just reason but wisdom is part of God's plan for us.

People tell us that it doesn't matter what we believe or think, but this is a satanic lie. Lives and entire cultures that are built on false ideas always degenerate. Wrong thinking eventually leads to wrong doing. Find a person living a destitute and degraded life in the street, and you can trace his or her condition back to what that person believes and thinks. Watch a talented Hollywood star experience one troubled marriage after another, eventually ending up alone, and you'll come to understand something about what that person believes or thinks. Consider the racial, ethnic, and religious wars of Rwanda, Bosnia, Kosovo, or Northern Ireland, and you can trace the fighting to what these people believe and think. Observe a brilliant and talented president of the United States risk his presidency and his legacy on astoundingly immature moral choices, and you will know what he really believes and thinks. Ideas have consequences, so it does indeed matter what we think.

God commands Christians in Philippians 4:8 to think on certain godly virtues. In Romans 12:2 God tells us not to be conformed to the pattern of this world but to be transformed by the renewing of our minds. Salvation is just the beginning. "Nor is any individual conversion complete until a Christian mind is formed within. To bring our every thought into captivity to Christ, to think Christianly, to see all of life in relationship to the Creator and Lord of all, this is not an optional appendage of secondary importance, but is at the very heart of what it means to be Christian."[5]

Avoiding conformity to the world or culture presupposes a transformed and renewed mind. To be transformed and renewed, a Christian's mind must be developed with a Christian worldview. This worldview is a philosophy of life that

- begins with personal faith in Jesus Christ as Savior and Lord
- acknowledges the sovereign character of God
- grows in the grace and knowledge of God's Word
- understands creation, the fall, and the Lord Jesus' work of redemption and reconciliation
- applies this knowledge to an understanding of the times and the material and moral order in which we live

Developing a Christian worldview may not be easy, but it is exciting. Through a Christian worldview we're privileged to learn God's will and to see it come to life through his Word applied in his world. That was the experience of Martin Luther, John Calvin, William Wilberforce, Abraham Kuyper, Elisabeth Elliot, C. Everett Koop, and others. When we live on the basis of a Christian worldview, we can learn to deal with social change while building culture and winning others to Christ.

LOVING OUR NEIGHBORS

The second great commandment is this: "Love your neighbor as yourself" (Matt. 22:39; Mark 12:31). Aside from loving God with all of our heart, soul, mind, and strength, we are to love our neighbors as much as we naturally love ourselves.

There are five Hebrew words for *neighbor,* and only one means "housed around" or "bounded property." The rest, like the one found in Leviticus 19:18, mean "an associate, friend, brother, companion, fellow, husband, lover." In the New Testament, the phrase "love your neighbor as yourself" is used nine times. Two Greek words for *neighbor,* used a total of five times, mean "housed around" or "adjoining one's ground." All other usages of the word *neighbor* employ a Greek

word meaning "close by, fellow, Christian, associate, friend, countryman, man, companion, or stranger."[6] In other words, our neighbors are not just those in our local neighborhood.

Jesus took the concept of neighbor one step further, saying, "You
have heard that it was said, 'Love your neighbor and hate your
enemy.' But I tell you: Love your enemies and pray for those who
persecute you, that you may be sons of your Father in heaven"
(Matt. 5:43–45). Jesus corrected what the religious Jews had taught
and restored the command to its original, broader Old Testament
meaning.

Our neighbors are our fellow men and women. Romans 12:10 tells
us to show brotherly love and to honor one another above ourselves.
In Romans 12:13 we're commanded, "Share with God's people who
are in need. Practice hospitality." In Romans 13:8 God says, "He who
loves his fellowman has fulfilled the law"; and again in verses 9–10,
"Love your neighbor as yourself. Love does no harm to its neighbor."
In James 1:27 we're directed to care for a certain kind of neighbor—
the fatherless and widows. In James 2:1–9 we're reminded that God
does not approve of favoritism.

Our neighbors are all human beings, regardless of race, ethnicity,
nationality, or gender. Acts 17:26 reminds us, "From one man he
made every nation of men, that they should inhabit the whole earth;
and he determined the times set for them and the exact places where
they should live."

For Christians, God's Word is even more pointed:

> You, my brothers, were called to be free. But do not use your free-
> dom to indulge the sinful nature; rather, serve one another in love.
> The entire law is summed up in a single command: "Love your
> neighbor as yourself." If you keep on biting and devouring each
> other, watch out or you will be destroyed by each other.
>
> Galatians 5:13–15

Loving our neighbors, no matter what neighborhood they live
in, is a biblically Christian theme. "If anyone says, 'I love God,' yet
hates his brother, he is a liar. . . . Whoever loves God must also love
his brother" (1 John 4:20–21).

CULTURAL CHRISTIANITY

How Christians love our neighbors and how we behave are directly linked to what we believe and how we think. How we react to the social changes around us and how well we make choices regarding cultural forms, methods, and practices depend on how attuned we are to God's will as expressed in his Word. Christians who have learned God's will and allowed the Holy Spirit to direct their lives will behave like Christ-followers. Christians who have not learned God's Word and who do not submit to the Holy Spirit's work in their lives will behave like the world.

So *don't confuse the way Christians behave with biblical Christianity.* I wish that I didn't have to say that, but it's true. More than once I've said this to non-Christians who earlier in life were burned by poorly behaving Christians or Christians who were overzealous in their drive to "get 'em saved." Christians don't always act Christianly. It's true for me, and, if you're a Christian, it's true for you. We don't always live in accordance with the teachings and values of the Bible. We disobey God. To put it bluntly, we sin.

Christians are sinners saved by grace. Praise God! But sometimes the sin is more evident than the grace. Think about racism as just one example. Have you ever considered what an incredible oxymoron it is to admit that some people are "Christian racists"? Christianity by its very nature is cosmopolitan, promoting the unity of the human race and brotherhood of all Christians.[7] Racism is a direct affront to the biblical teaching that all people are made in God's image. Yet I have heard some of the more dedicated and otherwise faithful Christians I know use derisive racial slurs. How can this be? Apparently these Christians were never challenged to apply their Christian faith to their attitudes about race.

Years ago I hired a person to work in our Christian college who was married interracially. Christians called me, questioning the wisdom of this appointment, some even going so far as to suggest that there was something sinful about the marriage. What interested me at the time was that none of these callers credited the many years of faithful Christian marriage this couple modeled, nor did they comprehend how ironic (some would say hypocritical) it was for them to criticize a healthy interracial marriage while single-race Christian marriages were regularly ending in divorce.

I've seen "Christian racism" expressed in other ways: jokes—supposedly harmless but often harsh, biting, even cruel expressions about racial differences that Christians whisper to one another at church fellowships. I've heard such jokes on Christian college campuses and I've heard them at pastors' gatherings. Now let me ask you something. Would these jokes be told if persons of another race or ethnic group were present? Would a person of another race even come to such Christian gatherings if he or she knew racial jokes were part of the mix? Would a person of another race even be welcome? Jesus was a Jew. Would he be welcome?

God condemns "foolish talk or coarse joking, which are out of place" (Eph. 5:4). He created all human beings, and he loves us all. This biblical truth is taught in the childhood chorus, "Red and yellow, black and white, they are precious in his sight. Jesus loves the little children of the world." Children seem to understand this truth, and we should learn from them.

And, by the way, racism is not just a white problem. Other races and ethnic groups evidence their own spiritual struggles with this very human failing.

Despite certain progress toward racial harmony since the 1960s, racism remains one of the most insidious sins in the world (including the Christian community) today. Yet you will go a long time in many if not most evangelical churches before you hear racism mentioned, let alone hear a sermon focusing on it.

A Cultural Church

Racism among Christians is just one reason for my saying don't confuse the way Christians behave with biblical Christianity. Christian people yield to sin. We develop our own interpretations of the world and of life rather than accepting God's interpretation. Often we do this for what we believe are the right motives. Then we build our worship of God and our church or religious practices around *our* philosophy and not God's teaching. Instead of a biblical or New Testament church, we've created a cultural church.

Christians can also develop a cultural church simply with the passage of time. Sinful choices may not have been involved originally, just cultural preferences and practices that in time take on a life of their own. They become traditions. After a while these traditions may no longer evidence any recognizable root in biblical principle, and the traditions themselves may take on sacred status. Fidelity to Christianity is determined on the basis of fidelity to the sacred practices—to the traditions—whether these traditions are biblical or not. When this happens, the transformation is complete, and the traditions have displaced, and maybe even replaced, the Scriptures. Either way, with or without wrong motives, a cultural church develops.

A cultural church is a place of religiosity, or what some call churchianity, not biblical Christianity. Even though a varying number of threads of biblically Christian practice may be evident in the cultural church tapestry, the picture that emerges looks more like the surrounding culture than like biblical Christianity.

Testing Cultural Practices

Now I don't want to be guilty of either overstating or understating this problem. Cultural influence on people and therefore on the church and religious practice is a given. No matter who we are and where we live in the world, we always live in a culture. Not all humanly generated cultural practices are evil, nor are they all good. All cultural practices must be tested by a biblically Christian faith.

Therein lies the difficulty. It's too easy, just too human, to simply accept the values and lifestyle practices handed to us by our culture rather than test them against God's Word. Because the Bible is supposed to be our base, the problem becomes more sinister when everyone begins doing his or her own thing. Then the church grows off base.

For centuries Christians have wrestled with their proper relationship to culture. Ascetics denied themselves all manner of normal human needs in a misguided attempt to reach a higher or deeper spiritual plane. Monks in medieval monasteries and nuns in cloisters separated themselves so completely from society that in most cases they (with the notable exception of Martin Luther whose newly discovered Christian faith revolutionized his outlook on virtually everything) made little impact on the course of human events.

Present-day Old Order Amish and some Mennonites try to withdraw in varying degrees from contemporary culture or at least much of its lifestyle, as do some within conservative evangelical and Pentecostal movements. (Many groups that do not espouse Christian faith also withdraw—some of these coalescing around environmental or antitechnology or anticorporate views. They live in communes and in general articulate a list of nonbiblical perspectives.)

For those who withdraw from culture, "the old familiar ways are more comfortable, less demanding, and less time consuming."[8] Many in these groups and myriad others like them become so proficient at withdrawing from culture that they develop a profound *isolation* from the people of their day.

A lot of theologically conservative churches fall into this trap. They tend to identify—indeed equate—their own selected lifestyle choices (including sometimes even secular, anti-Christian views) with biblical Christianity. In some cases they yield to *legalism* and then offer the non-Christian an either/or choice: Be like us or you aren't going to heaven.

Among the more theologically liberal churches, the danger is not isolation but *accommodation*. During the twentieth century alone we've witnessed the theological liberalism of mainline churches, neo-orthodoxy, and liberation theology, all of which have been immersed in the forms, methods, and lifestyle choices of Modernity. Theologically liberal churches tend to identify so much with contemporary culture (including sometimes even secular, anti-Christian views) that they lose their distinctiveness, in some cases yield to license, and then offer the non-Christian little that is different from common culture.

As you can see, many liberal and conservative churches make the same mistake, albeit for very different reasons. They become cultural churches and lose their prophetic voice. Liberals *identify* with current culture. Conservatives *isolate or insulate* themselves from current culture, frequently creating their own subcultures. Neither approach is ultimately effective in God's command to *interact* with culture.

So what would Jesus do?

THE "IN THE WORLD/ NOT OF THE WORLD" TENSION

In the New Testament Book of John, chapter 17, we can find the answer. In this passage of Scripture God recorded for us the true "Lord's prayer." It's the prayer Jesus prayed just before his arrest, trials, and crucifixion. He knew what he was facing, but he spent most of his time praying for his followers rather than for himself.

Jesus observes that Christians are in the world, but he wants them to be not of the world (v. 14). Then in the same prayer he seems to contradict himself and say Christians should go into the world (v. 18). What did he mean by this? It's simple, really, but powerful.

We live our lives in the world by virtue of *creation* (our physical beings) and *culture* (our way of life). But God does not want us to live our lives based on values and practices generated by human culture.[9] He expects us to be *not of the world* by being identifiably different or distinctive via our *re-creation* (rebirth or salvation in Christ) and our work to *transform culture*. In turn, he commands us to go *into the world* and both develop and influence culture with Christian values—what Christians call the *Cultural Mandate* from the Book of Genesis—as well as win others to Christ in this world— what Christians call the *Great Commission* from the Book of Matthew.

"In the world, not of the world" and "into the world" are parts of God's answer to Francis A. Schaeffer's question, "How shall we then live?"[10] God did not leave us without guidance for our cultural existence. Jesus cared and still cares about how we live. He prayed specifically for those of us who follow him today: "I pray also for those who will believe in me through their message, that all of them may be one" (John 17:20–21). He wanted us to learn to live properly in this world: "My prayer is not that you take them out of the world but that you protect them from the evil one. They are not of the world, even as I am not of it. Sanctify them by the truth; your word is truth" (vv. 15–17).

While God wants us to be different from the world, he put us in the world for a purpose. This is what I call the "in the world/not of the world tension." It's a tension from which we'll never escape. Some try to escape it by drifting into license and others try to avoid it by embracing legalism, but neither approach works. As long as we live, we live in a culture—yet we're commanded to lead lives that are distinctively different from others in that culture. It's a spiritual tension God intended, for it allows us to exercise free will, responsibility, and love for his glory.

SALT AND LIGHT

God does not want Christians to be invisible or even low profile. He doesn't want us to be non-impact people. He's given us the gospel, the Good News, the greatest, most celebrated cause in all of history. We are his ambassadors for truth. Metaphorically speaking, God wants us to be both salt and light in this world (Matt. 5:13–16). As salt, we're warned against losing our distinctiveness. Our presence in the world should be noticeable. Our Christian values should "flavor" our culture. As light, we're commanded, "Let your light shine before men, that they may see your good deeds and praise your Father in heaven" (v. 16). Our presence in the world should challenge the darkness that sin and Satan bring. Christ's light shining through us should point the way to the Savior.

Now here's the point: How can we be salt and light in the world if we're confused and overwhelmed by social change, laden with our own rules and traditions, or distracted by culture wars within the Christian family? The answer is simple—we can't. Something's got to change.

In this book I'll develop nine principles for living a God-honoring Christian life in rapidly changing times:

1. We must affirm biblical Christianity and personal, saving faith in Jesus Christ.
2. We must develop a biblically Christian worldview, which yields spiritual discernment.
3. We must learn to anticipate change as much as order, for both are part of God's sovereign design for this world.
4. We must recognize that biblical Christianity is not about rules but about a relationship with Christ.
5. We must work to evangelize the lost, edify the saints, and transform the culture for the cause of Christ.
6. We must create culture by developing the potential of Postmodernity and ministering to its problems.
7. We must combat postmodernism, particularly its moral relativism.
8. We must model biblical community in the Christian church.
9. We must go into the world, speaking the truth in love.

1

CHANGING TIMES

Now What?

God blessed them and said to them, "Be fruitful and increase in number; fill the earth and subdue it. Rule over the fish of the sea and the birds of the air and over every living creature that moves on the ground."

Genesis 1:28

Therefore go and make disciples of all nations, baptizing them in the name of the Father and of the Son and of the Holy Spirit, and teaching them to obey everything I have commanded you. And surely I am with you always, to the very end of the age.

Matthew 28:19–20

T he Three Stooges, Curly, Larry, and Moe—sometimes accompanied by Curly Joe or Shemp—dominated early cinema and television with their uproarious slapstick comedy. They stumbled from one adventure to the next, made noise, embarrassed those around them, and created generalized chaos, yet always in the end they got the girl, did something worthy, and emerged the lovable heroes. They were considered so funny that they became Hollywood stars, made a great living, and were mimicked by countless people who applied the Stooges' phrases and behavior to every-day life.

But aside from a few people who still appreciate the Three Stooges' "classic" humor, most people today no longer consider the Stooges very funny. In fact now their physical comedy looks harsh or even mean, their antics appear infantile, and their jokes seem lame or even boring. Aside from the fact that these gentlemen have gone on to their reward, what happened?

Culture changed. The Three Stooges simply no longer connect with contemporary values, attitudes, and social conditions. They're no more relevant to the current spirit of the age than the Keystone Kops or knights in shining armor. If you are a comedian today, you've got to figure out a new way to be funny so you can be successful. If you're a Christian, you've got to figure out how to relate to your changing culture in a way that honors God.

Cultural Homework

Christians have work to do—homework. It's a history assignment from God. In the Bible's Book of Genesis, chapter 1, verse 28, God gave all human beings his *Cultural Mandate*. People must develop, influence, even transform human culture in a manner that glorifies God. This command dates to the Garden of Eden and has never been rescinded. It encompasses all the activities of every man, woman, and child from Adam and Eve to you and me to the newest newborn.

In Matthew 28:19–20 God gave all Christians a second assignment, his *Great Commission*. Christians must go and make disciples of all nations, teaching them to obey everything that God commanded. Being a representative of God in this world is the Christian's prime directive. It's what we're supposed to do. God expects Christians to be about his work throughout all of human history and in all human culture.

Culture is our way of life:

> that activity of man, the image bearer of God, by which he fulfills the creation mandate to cultivate the earth, to have dominion over it and to subdue it. . . . Culture, then, is any and all human effort and labor expended upon the cosmos, to unearth its treasures and its

riches and bring them into the service of man for the enrichment of human existence unto the glory of God.[1]

God made each of us with the ability to reason. We can think. We're rational, and we occupy a place in the cosmos a little lower than heavenly beings (Ps. 8:5). With that kind of pedigree we should not be formed by culture. In other words, culture should not create us; we should create culture.

Human beings *precede* culture and *create* culture as an expression of their religious faith. Culture is what we do with the creation God gave us—work, play, music, entertainment, clothing, diet, everything. What we do with the creation God gave us and why we do it depends directly on our religious views. That's why T. S. Eliot said culture is "lived religion."[2] Consequently, every culture crisis is a crisis of character, the result of apostasy from true faith.[3]

THE POSTMODERN PROBLEM

The early twenty-first century is a battleground for this kind of culture crisis, understood as two great culture wars. One is a macro culture war for the character and soul of human society, and thus the nation. The other is a micro culture war for the character and soul of the Christian community, or what we may call the church. The national culture war is the product of philosophic naturalism and its cousin, a generally accepted moral relativism that emphasizes subjectivity as the arbiter of morality and reality.

Naturalism, a rejection of the supernatural, particularly the God of the Bible, has become the dominant motif of our times. It's the idea that nothing can be known that we cannot test with our five senses. If you can't see, taste, hear, smell, or touch it, then it doesn't exist. Clearly, if there is no belief in a sovereign God and his standards, the door is open for a morality of human choice or a morality of the moment. As Fyodor Dostoyevsky described it, "If God is dead, everything is permitted."[4] G. K. Chesterton later paraphrased this comment, noting that when God is dead, people do not believe in nothing; they believe in anything.[5] Without God, nothing remains in every form of human endeavor but moral relativism, and this religious assumption defines an emerging mentality that is dominating the period of time now being called Postmodernity.

The Christian culture war is the product of an underdeveloped Christian worldview resulting in a practical ambiguity that confuses doctrine and dogma and ignores Christian liberty. A Christian worldview grounded in biblical revelation fosters a spiritual discernment capable of distinguishing truth from error, the consequential from the inconsequential, and the harmless from the harmful. A Christian worldview is the "full armor of God" with which we are able to "stand firm" (Eph. 6:10–18).

In both the macro and the micro culture wars there are individuals and groups who claim a form of godliness but deny its power (2 Tim. 3:5). Both culture wars result from a denial of divine transcendence. God apparently isn't who he claims to be.

The macro culture war can be seen in national debates over the politics of meaning, family values, or the politics of virtue, and in a gradual disappearance of an agreed on public attitude toward what is right or wrong—what were once considered the most fundamental beliefs of Western society. The macro culture war is also evident in a host of worldview battles pertaining to abortion, biomedical ethics, and evolutionary theory, and especially in a growing acceptance, even promotion, of sexually deviant morality.

The micro culture war can be seen in myriad Christian debates over church worship format, preaching styles, music, fashion, and entertainment, which have caused internecine church splits, and especially in the disappearance of a common view among biblical churches concerning sexually moral behavior. The Christian culture war is different from yet related to and even influenced by the national culture war.

The national culture war is rooted in moral relativism, the idea that God is irrelevant, so truth does not exist. The Christian culture war is rooted in theological ambiguity, the idea that God is relevant only if he fits our definition of him. The national culture war results from putting God outside our philosophic box. The Christian culture war results from putting God inside our philosophic box. Both perspectives miss the point that we are to worship God in spirit and in truth. Both miss the point that "It is the Lord Christ you are serving" (Col. 3:24).

How do Christians survive this? Better yet, how do we thrive in this time of great change? Do we send an e-mail addressed to

God@Heaven.divine? Do we say to each other, "You're okay; I'm okay; it'll all be okay"? (It's difficult to get three lies into one sentence, but there are three in that last one.) Do we develop Christian schizophrenia, a split spiritual personality with part believing God and part wondering if Christianity is really true?

Certainly one thing we cannot do is respond to postmodern culture with what Os Guinness calls a "Sunday school–level faith in a university-level society." If you've ever searched for a church to join that offered more than Sunday school–level teaching, you probably know what I mean. In New York a few years ago, about forty-five minutes from the Big Apple, my family began what turned out to be an eighteen-month search for a Bible-believing, Bible-teaching church.

The first church we selected had no youth program. So, as the father of four young children, after about three months, I asked the pastor when they were going to start a youth program. He said, "When we get more youth, we'll start a program." I was just a visiting newcomer at that point, so I refrained from saying what crossed my mind: *That's not how it's done.* This pastor and consequently the church evidenced no vision whatsoever for the hundreds of young people populating the suburbs around them. He preached, but he didn't connect with his community. So we left the church. A few months later, so did he.

Our stay at the next church lasted about two months. The pastor, who held a doctoral degree in theology from a distinguished seminary, preached fifteen-minute sermons limited on Scripture and laden with platitudes, which had no perceptible application to anything that was happening in our lives, in the city, or in culture at large. The same was true of the Sunday school class. The teacher did not teach; he facilitated, which is to say that he acted as moderator of a discussion in which everyone pooled their own ignorance of the Scripture: "I don't really *feel* that God could send snakes to discipline the Israelites." Or, "Surely Moses didn't lead that many people into the wilderness; the Bible must be exaggerating a bit there."

The straw that broke our camel's back came a week before Christmas when I retrieved our children from the youth program only to learn that biblical teaching had been set aside in favor of making peanut brittle with the older children and making a Rudolph the Red-Nosed Reindeer hand puppet with the little ones. I'm not against candy or Rudolph, but these things in the absence of bibli-

cal instruction could not prepare our children for a spiritually conflicted world.

Our stay at the next church lasted longer, and our youngest even
accepted Christ as a result of this church's ministry. For this we are
grateful. The young pastor and his wife were kind and dedicated,
serious about their calling. They were "good Christian people." But
he had been taught in seminary that the Christian life was pretty
much summarized in evangelism. His sermons were filled with hell-
fire and brimstone and at first were a pleasant antidote to the shallow platitudes we'd heard in our previous church. At least we were
thumbing the Scriptures again. He gave an invitation every service,
but after a while we realized the same people were going forward
week after week.

One Sunday after we returned home, I said to my wife, "You
know, Pastor would be happiest if we got saved every Sunday." Same
sermon, different text. There were salvation altar calls every week
but no preaching about growth in the grace and knowledge of the
Word and no application to what was being reported in the *New York
Times*. We left that church.

Finally, we found a church with a spiritually mature pastor who
preached "the whole counsel of God" and who loved the Lord, loved
his people, and encouraged us to go out and live a godly life in God's
world. This fellowship became our church home during the next
many months of our New York tour of duty before God moved us
west. The pastor is now with our Lord, but during his life on earth
he wisely worked to edify those under his care and send us out to
do God's work in the world. His ministry, and therefore the church's
ministry, was to help us dig deep into the Scriptures and learn to
apply them to our lives, every part of our lives. Whatever *Newsweek*
was reporting, whatever trends seemed to be developing in culture,
whatever concerns were identified in the members of the church,
they found their way into the pastor's sermons. By example as much
as statement, he demonstrated that the Christian faith is relevant both
to our Christian lives and to the lives of our non-Christian neighbors. We learned God's will for his church because the pastor shared
his Christian worldview, his belief that God's people must live by the
Scriptures and live out what they learn in the world.

God's will for us expressed in the Cultural Mandate and the Great
Commission is a call to action. People need to *be* something—a child
of God by grace through faith in Jesus Christ. Christian people need

to *know* something—the truth of God's revelation of his moral will. And Christians need to *do* something—live out their unchanging biblical faith in a rapidly changing world, which is the call of God.

RAPIDLY CHANGING TIMES

Social change is a fact of history. During our time, it's been rapid social change. No, strike that. *Very* rapid social change. No, that's not it either. I-can't-change-fast-enough-to-keep-up-with-yesterday-let-alone-tomorrow social change is now an unavoidable fact of contemporary life. Try as we may, we can't escape it. And it's not just the funny quotient of the Three Stooges that has changed. Nothing—or at least it seems that way—stays the same.

People have been talking about change for a while. In his nineteenth-century masterpiece *A Tale of Two Cities,* Charles Dickens eloquently said:

> It was the best of times, it was the worst of times, it was the age of wisdom, it was the age of foolishness, it was the epoch of belief, it was the epoch of incredulity, it was the season of Light, it was the season of Darkness, it was the spring of hope, it was the winter of despair, we had everything before us, we had nothing before us . . .

Perhaps the beginning of the twenty-first century can reasonably be described as both the best and worst of times. But in this age of moral relativism and a rejection of the very idea of truth, can anyone really claim that the dominant worldview of this time offers wisdom, light, and hope? I don't think so. In Dickens's time intellectuals still believed in a better tomorrow. Today they're not even sure there will be a tomorrow. This may sound exaggerated to you, but test me. Listen to avant-garde music or tour the postmodern section of the local art museum. You'll soon understand what I mean. There is no truth, no meaning, no hope, just cynicism and despair.

Christians know better. But we're too busy tilting at our own cultural windmills to fight the real enemy. Christians spend more time fussing with each other over minor cultural practices than we do creating or reforming culture. So far we've been more *reactive* than *proactive.*

The twentieth century was marked by more social change more rapidly experienced than perhaps any other time of history. Now our "normal" is more rapid social change. Prospects for the beginning of the twenty-first century suggest that if anything changes about social change it will be that change will happen even more rapidly. Rapid social change is now the typical experience of life. But a lot of people (and, you guessed it, Christians in particular) haven't figured that out.

Most of us would rather avoid change altogether (especially aging). We're creatures of habit. Sameness is familiar, therefore comforting. Sameness may be bland, but it's friendly by definition. Routine is more to our liking. We don't have to think. There's no cognitive dissonance to rattle our equilibrium. We just react. Depending on the circumstance, that can be a good or a not-so-good thing.

Change, on the other hand, is usually unsettling—at least for a lot of folks. Change is a destabilizer. It often confuses and disorients people. For some people it's downright scary. By definition, change means that things are different, and that creates uncertainty.

Unlike routine, change forces us to think. Our uncertainty grows when behaviors that fit an earlier time don't seem appropriate in a new situation. Social change loosens our sense of ourselves, even our values. Change puts pressure on our belief systems. What we thought we knew may need to be rethought. This is true for the interpreters of biblical Christianity as well as for those of any other historic belief.

Marvin Mayers writes: "Since biblical Christianity is a dynamic process born in a changing setting and since it introduces change in the life of individuals and society, it resists being bound by the narrow ethnocentric and restrictive legalisms that often characterize the established church. Thus there arises in each generation a reformation."[6] In other words, the arrival of new choices, both in social and personal life, often makes the memorized responses of our parents' generation—let alone our grandparents' point of view— untenable.

Sadly, in the face of this kind of change, some people reject Christian belief not because Christian belief has failed but because believers have not applied its teachings in practical ways to the new situation. While it is clearly not accurate to say that no Christians apply their faith to culture in a way that honors God, it is eminently apparent that a majority of Christians have struggled mightily in the face of rapid social change. Consequently, opportunities for advancing God's kingdom in this potentially exciting era are lost because Christians are overwhelmed by change and are not in a position to influence it.

LOOKING FOR ZACCHAEUS

The single greatest obstacle to the church's fulfillment of both the Cultural Mandate and the Great Commission is the inability of Christians to learn to deal with social change. When we should be engaging, influencing, and possibly transforming culture, we run from it. Social change has us baffled. When we should be armed with the Word of God and fighting sin and Satan, we are armed with our personal prejudices and fighting each other. When we should be confident in our Christian faith, bearing witness of its truth in the face of all other alternative worldviews, we cower before the other worldviews. When we should be "looking for Zacchaeus" in the marketplace and winning neighbors to Christ, we are withdrawn into our church subcultures for fear of being tainted by the world. But Zacchaeus doesn't come to the church anymore. He's in the world, in his own neighborhood, "up a tree" of his own making. We'll never reach him if we don't go looking for him. But even if we find him, we won't be able to speak his language because we don't understand the changing world in which he lives.[7]

Do you realize how much Christian jargon characterizes our speech? What does *fellowship* mean to a nonbeliever? What about *born again, clergy,* or *laity?* Would your non-Christian neighbors understand you if you said, "I'll meet you in the vestibule (or narthex)"? What is a backslider? What does the worship leader mean when he says, "Give someone a holy hug"? Do your non-Christian neighbors know what you mean when you talk about daily bread or devotions? Or if you said, "God *led* me to do this," would they understand? Our language fits our subculture, not theirs. Learning to communicate is key to our witness and influence.

Now let's turn it around. Do you know what your non-Christian neighbor means when she says, "I'm religious; I've always been religious"? Or, "I really hammered myself the other night on the way home"? What about, "I'm a Scorpio"?

Right after the Berlin Wall fell in 1989, I traveled with a group of Christian educators to the Soviet Union. For the first three days we were amazed at how many people told us, "I'm a believer. I believe in God." We thought, *Are there this many Christians in Russia?* It took us a while to discern that what they really meant was, "I am not one of those godless Communists you've heard about." They meant what we would mean if we said, "They're religious." Once this became clear to us, we began to gently tell them about the special meaning that Christians assign to the word *believer*. We need to learn Zacchaeus's language.

A CHRISTIAN WORLDVIEW CRISIS

A Christian worldview, grounded in the lordship of Jesus Christ and biblical revelation, is missing in most Christians' lives, and this lack is the source of the church's inability to deal with social change. In the next chapter we'll discuss how Christians can develop their Christian worldview, but for now you should know that a Christian worldview is an understanding, based on biblical principles and values, of all of the world and life. Further, a Christian worldview is most effective when it is applied to everything we experience. We are to model biblically Christian values, to enact them in cultural practice, and to "speak the truth in love" to spiritually lost and dying neighbors. A biblically constructed Christian worldview is the only comprehensive framework of reality that actually fits with reality. It speaks to all of life. It makes sense. It works. It can be tested and found trustworthy. It explains both good and evil, and it provides truthful answers for our quest for meaning and significance. That's why the church's failure to teach a biblically Christian worldview greatly undermines the ability of Christians to engage culture and understand social change in a manner that fulfills God's will. That's why Satan is pleased.

Terry Crist describes the dilemma. He says that for too long Christians have

> sat down at [the] table of unilateral disarmament with the enemy and said to him, in effect, "Don't bother us and we won't bother you! You can have the kingdoms of this world—entertainment, the arts, media, politics, athletics, law, economics—and we will take our Sunday school programs, Bible clubs, Christian conferences and home

Bible studies. If you leave us alone, we'll leave you alone." And we bargained off God's property! Because of our desire to escape the challenges of this life, we have held a century-long fire sale, liquidating our interests and influence in all of popular culture.[8]

We must understand that "genuine Christianity is more than a relationship with Jesus as expressed in personal piety, church attendance, Bible study, and works of charity. It is more than discipleship, more than believing a system of doctrines about God. Genuine Christianity is a way of seeing and comprehending all reality. It is a worldview."[9] Living our Christian faith includes all of these practices, but a more fully developed understanding of biblical revelation's relevance to this world is also essential.

The unbiblical worldviews at work in postmodern culture are going largely unchallenged. Well-presented Christian truth, applicable to the issues raised, is missing. It's not missing in action; it's missing from action. Counterfeit worldviews are winning the battle for men and women's minds by default. They are winning, not because Christians aren't witnessing to the nonbeliever, but because Christians cannot answer some of the nonbeliever's bigger questions.

But we ought to be able to answer these questions. We possess the truth. Through the Spirit's enabling, a Christian worldview increases our spiritual discernment, allowing us to "test the spirits to see whether they are from God" (1 John 4:1). In a Christian worldview, there is no dichotomy between the sacred and the secular, for God's moral law exists for all of life. Nothing is beyond his concern or his control. This most certainly encompasses all social change, as well as humanity's attempts at culture without him. And this includes Christians and our sometimes culturally confused attempts to build his church.

THE CHRISTIAN CULTURE WARS

The church has too frequently equated its forms and methods with the essence of Christianity. In other words, Christians have asserted that what they do in their particular church *is* Christianity. As a direct result, no matter where you go, you'll find Christian people who are fussing, fuming, and fighting with each other. We're "biting and devouring each other," in danger of being "destroyed by each other" (Gal. 5:15). Over what?

The turbulence brought about by rapid social change causes us to hold on tightly to our comfort-giving, habitual forms, methods, and practices. They become our port in the storm. Rather than grab on to the eternal principles of Scripture and apply them in a new and relevant way, which is what a well-developed Christian world-view enables us to do, we hold on to our familiar cultural practices. Then we fight with others who are doing the same thing. When this happens, our Christian testimony is lost to the world, and we rapidly become anachronistic to the rapidly changing culture.

Sometimes these battles center on doctrinal debates, which have taken place throughout the history of Christianity and are recognized by the church as legitimate discussions of belief. Much more often in this era, though, church conflicts focus on cultural issues, matters of choice and preference born in a rapidly changing social environment. I'm talking about music, church service worship formats, clothing, entertainment, hairstyles and other matters of personal appearance, and much more.

I know of a church in the state of Michigan that split because the people could not agree on whether to allow contemporary music styles. I know of another church in a southern state in which women are not permitted to wear slacks to services. Still another church lost many families when the pastor and church leadership decided to schedule a nontraditional seeker service, not on Sunday but on a different night of the week. I've known churches in which men had to cut their hair a certain length to be allowed to sing in the choir. One church in Iowa won't allow guitars, while another in the same state won't allow organs. I've read church constitutions that deny membership to people who smoke or otherwise use tobacco or drink any alcohol. Some fundamentalist churches have staked their claim to faith on the King James Version of the Bible, considering all other versions a form of apostasy. I've talked with many pastors who became victims of church culture wars, some of whom left the ministry in disillusionment.

Christian people who identify their choices of forms, methods, lifestyle, and practice as the *only* truly biblical and Christian way of doing things usually create their own "holy list." This practice is common among Christian churches of virtually every denomination. A Christian or group of Christians begins to judge other Christians' spirituality on the basis of their list. This attitude implies, of course, that if you don't make the same choices, you're not spiritual, not biblical, and maybe not even Christian. What begins as a preference shifts to a presumptuous, even arrogant attitude of "my way is the only way." It's the Christian's version of political, or should I say spiritual, correctness. Not long after the holy lists are created, the Christian culture wars begin.

These Christian culture wars have split churches, schools, mission agencies, even families, along with just about every other form of Christian enterprise you can name. People align themselves against each other in their own version of a civil war. Meanwhile the real enemies—sin, Satan, and his counterfeit religious worldviews—advance virtually uncontested.

The intriguing but grievous part about all this is that it's so unnecessary—and sinful. God did not put us into a changing world without telling us something about who he is or how to evaluate whether change is good, bad, or indifferent. Or dare I say it? God did not leave us without telling us how to *allow others* to be different and maybe even how we might learn to *enjoy* morally appropriate social change or different cultural practices. In the unchanging principles of the Word of God, he gave us exactly what we need.

BORN AGAIN FREE

Social change might give us fits, but it wouldn't be nearly the problem it's been if Christians practiced the teachings of biblical Christianity. Since the church has not developed its understanding of a biblically Christian worldview, it has become more inward focused—privatized. Consequently, the church has gradually lost its cultural foothold and become progressively more marginalized from the issues plaguing our times. First modern then postmodern culture has been all too willing to accommodate this shift.

Christians living without a Christian worldview or with an undeveloped Christian worldview create a church less prepared to address life in community. Without a biblically defined Christian worldview the church has no means of balancing the inevitable tensions of the one and the many or unity and diversity. If the church does not live by biblical norms for unity and diversity, then either unity or diversity eventually assumes a dominant position. The church may drift toward a maximized unity—meaning individuality is almost impossible to maintain as everyone is expected to subscribe to the party line on all matters of practice. Or the church gradually embraces a maximized diversity—meaning community is almost impossible to maintain as individuals pursue whatever seems right in their own eyes. Both extremes generate Christian culture wars.

Scripture provides the perfect answer. A Christian worldview celebrates both community and individuality, balancing and integrating the two. This is pictured in both the family and the body of Christ, with the perfect example being the Trinity. God created us to live freely in community with the ability and responsibility to make choices, and he gave us the doctrine of Christian liberty to guide those choices.

Christian liberty is the biblical teaching that Christians have been provided with God-given moral commands ("everything we need for life and godliness" in 2 Peter 1:3) regarding a certain limited list of vitally important matters, like honesty or sexual morality, on which we can build our lives and culture. Beyond these "moral absolutes," God grants Christians the freedom to make judgments about what is best for their lives and culture.

But there's a problem. While Romans 14, along with other passages of Scripture, develops the doctrine of Christian liberty, the church seems to have skipped that part of the Bible. Christian liberty may be the least understood and least practiced biblical doctrine. Christian people have not grasped what it means to embrace a faith that is both transcultural, meaning that it applies to all cultures, and transhistorical, meaning that our faith applies to human cultures through all time. We haven't understood the implications of our spiritual gift of liberty, and we certainly haven't wanted to allow others to experience it.

This is not to say that everything done in the name of Christian liberty is legitimate and appropriate. Certainly God has not said this. But the Christian culture wars make it plain that Christians have a lot to learn about social change and their liberty in Christ. I'm saying that with a little effort we can learn what God has to say about social change and order, how we can live responsibly before him in history, and how we may even come to enjoy the incredible creativity (the differing ideas) that God has placed in the hearts of men and women made in his image.

All this means that Christians must go through a period of study, thought, and re-evaluation that will take much of our energy. Conflicts will arise within Christian circles as older people especially are not consciously aware of this need for re-orientation, and therefore think that the old answers are still valid and sufficient. It is not that the foundation has to change, or that the basic doctrines have lost their meaning. But the expression and formulation of them sometimes needs rethinking as we listen afresh to God's Word, and seek to present it to the new world in which we are now living.[10]

UNCHANGING TRUTH IN CHANGING TIMES

Contemporary culture is the product of religious worldviews and human actions inherited from social history and constructed by men and women living today. This rapidly changing culture, the "world" as the Bible calls it, is dominated by the prince and power of the air and a legion of non-Christian worldviews. These worldviews are pretenders to real faith, and every day they combat and compete with a Christian perspective. Our responsibility and privilege as Christians living in this age is to live out our Christian faith.

God has given Christians both the Cultural Mandate and the Great Commission. We are stewards of the world and of the Word. To please God, we must exercise our faith in him by caring for the world and carrying forth the Word. Because we know God, the unchanging Creator and sustainer of the universe and the author of the Bible, his eternal Word, social change is not a threat to us. It's an opportunity. It should not cause us to insulate ourselves in cocoons of ritual and tradition, but rather it should encourage us to apply our biblical faith vigorously, knowing that God's Word always makes an impact, never returning to him void.

Our challenge now is to develop our Christian worldview. Once we've learned this lesson, the homework assignment God gave us will be a lot more fun.

2

DEVELOPING A CHRISTIAN
WORLDVIEW

The fear of the Lord is the beginning of knowledge.

Proverbs 1:7

Men of Issachar . . . understood the times and knew what Israel should
do.

1 Chronicles 12:32

Early twenty-first-century culture offers us a moral and metaphysical smorgasbord—techno-paganism, environmental pantheism, limping institutional religions, moral pluralism, scientism, Darwinism, secularism, New Age philosophy, and a vigorously
emerging Islam. It's a time dominated by worldviews that are wolves
in sheep's clothing, lulling people into a false sense of security only
to lead them to destruction. Escapism is in. Substance abuse still
plagues us. Sexual promiscuity is more widespread than ever.

People believe in a god but not in God. Our modern-postmod-
ern culture is anything but secular. It's full of vogue but vague spiritualism, yet nothing seems to fill the hole in people's hearts. They
try by studying Deepak Chopra's "seven spiritual laws of success" or
being "embraced by the light" with Betty J. Eadie. They pursue reincarnation with Shirley MacLaine, Buddhism with Sharon Stone or

43

Richard Gere, or explore Christian Science with Tom Cruise, or simply call one of Dionne Warwick's late-night psychic hotlines. If none of this works, they can travel farther along the road less traveled with M. Scott Peck or look for a "celestine prophecy" with James Redfield.

There's more. Today we can try to identify our animal-spirit guide, experience prelife therapy, have our aura read, or examine soul retrieval with Kate Solisti and a host of other spiritualist gurus. We can even worship Sophie with radical feminists, some of whom equate marriage with slavery and all sex with rape. Or we can look to a new religion with L. Ron Hubbard and celebrities like John Travolta. As I said, there's a moral and metaphysical smorgasbord available.

Over and against this worldview cafeteria is biblical Christianity. God's truth has been revealed. We possess the Holy Writ. But it must be applied, and that's our job. If Christians expect to make a difference in our morally indifferent culture, we must develop a biblically Christian worldview. Without a Christian worldview, we will not be able to withstand the intellectual onslaught of nonbiblical worldviews now influencing our daily lives. Christians won't be able to answer the assertions and questions based on "reason without revelation" until we first develop our reason through biblical revelation.[1] Our first step toward loving God and our neighbors and toward cultural renewal is a Christian worldview.

EVERYONE HAS A WORLDVIEW

Everyone has a worldview, although most people either don't know it or don't reflect on it. We gain our worldview simply by being alive. God gives every individual certain abilities and talents at conception (this is nature). God made all people thinking, rational beings, able to act independently in this world. Yet most of what people become is learned behavior (this is nurture). Early in life and on into adulthood, in a kind of philosophic osmosis, we tend to absorb values and perspectives, even our most basic thoughts (presuppositions and fundamental assumptions about life and the world), from the world around us. It's typically a rather unthinking process, so much so that Francis A. Schaeffer once said that most of us catch presuppositions like we catch measles.[2] In other words, most people don't give much thought or effort to the development of their worldview. Nevertheless, everyone has a worldview.

A worldview is an understanding of the nature of reality, what Abraham Kuyper called a "life-system," a term that originates with the German *weltanschauung*.[3] It's a philosophic outlook that enables people to respond to their existence and their environment by providing them with a guide for their thoughts and actions. James W. Sire defined a worldview as "a set of presuppositions (assumptions which may be true, partially true, or entirely false) which we hold (consciously or subconsciously, consistently or inconsistently) about the basic makeup of our world."[4] People use this set of presuppositions as a guide to decision making, activities, and attitudes.

Because the world is full of information, we need a worldview in order to function well mentally. Our challenge is to relate in a meaningful way all the information we take in. If we're interested in unity or wholeness, or just in trying to understand anything, we need some kind of paradigm or framework in which to work. This paradigm or framework or grid or lens helps us view, organize, and interpret all that can be known. "A worldview is thus the confession of a unifying perspective, and this confessional character is true of secular and religious views alike."[5]

A worldview answers (or should answer) several questions:

1. Where are we, or what is the nature of the reality in which we find ourselves?
2. Who are we, or what is the nature and task of human beings?
3. What's wrong, or how do we understand and account for evil and brokenness?
4. What's the remedy, or how do we find a path through our brokenness to wholeness?[6]

A worldview should provide a wholeness or integrity that enables people to relate to all things in life, including faith and reason and the natural and supernatural (which some worldviews deny). Beyond this, a worldview helps us define what is good in life and is, thus, indispensable to living.

Many worldviews cannot answer the basic questions listed above, and some worldviews only answer them incompletely. Many are based in part on false assumptions; some are false in their entirety. In any case, it is clear that all people develop, hold, and use a worldview. All worldviews, irrespective of whether they may be considered true or false, share a common construction. Certain first principles, variously termed presuppositions, pre-theoretical commitments, first premises, faith perspectives, or faith assumptions, exist on which the worldview is built.[7] Identify these first principles and you'll understand the worldview.

First Principles

Certain presuppositions, or fundamental starting points, that a person believes to be true form the basis of that person's worldview. Presuppositions are *assumed truths* about all of the most basic yet profound questions of life. When we say "assumed truth," we're talking about faith. Every believer in a divine being, every agnostic, every atheist, and every type of philosopher alike has faith, whether he or she admits it or not. This is true because to think is to have faith in something.

Before people recognize or interpret facts (which by strict definition are things we know are true), they must first have a faith about facts.[8] This faith about facts forms the basis of each person's test of truth. What you interpret as fact depends on your faith about facts. We can say without fear of contradiction that human beings are inescapably religious, because everyone has a faith about certain facts.

The value and validity of these varied beliefs are determined not just by the fact of faith but by the *object* of that faith. Sanctimoniously saying, "I have faith" or "I'm a person of faith" doesn't mean much. It's a bit like saying, "I'm human" or "I breathe." The question is, faith in what?

Every person works with presuppositions (consciously or subconsciously) concerning the existence, nature, character, and revelation of God. This is the most essential and foundational element of human thought. Beginning with an understanding of God, every person then develops his or her worldview around certain other basic thoughts, among them the nature and destiny of humanity, the meaning and purpose of life, the nature of good and evil, the nature of the universe, and the method of gaining knowledge.

For example, a Marxist presupposes that God does not exist and that economics determines the course of human events. Consequently, for the Marxist, human beings are simply pawns of the system, and good and evil is an economic story of the "haves" and "have nots." Many scientists embrace naturalism, presupposing that only the natural world matters and that the supernatural is beyond knowing, irrelevant, or simply does not exist. Consequently, they reject biblical teachings about the Creator and attempt to attribute all that occurs in this world to natural causes. Since God does not exist in their worldview, morality is not determined by God's will but by power, biology, human choice, or some other source within the system.

Muslims presuppose that "there is no God but Allah and Muhammad is his prophet." They are monotheists, but their god has no partners (thus no Trinity), he does not beget (thus Jesus is not his Son), and he is responsible for good and evil. In the Islamic belief system, Allah is a god of fate and fear. He is arbitrary and even capricious in his dealings with human beings. Muslims, therefore, cannot fully explain concepts like love, forgiveness, or peace, because the meaning of these concepts depends on the existence of a God who is both righteous and loving and who defines forgiveness in the work of his Son, Jesus.

A businessman politician recently told me, "I'm not religious." Yet he is conservative in his political views, gives to children's causes, establishes scholarships for single mothers at area colleges, loves his wife, sometimes uses salty language, considers political office a public trust, and is quite proud of his financial success. All of these attitudes and actions are based on the religious character of what he believes is good, right, or true. This is what determines his choices. What he really meant to say was that he doesn't go to church, doesn't think that he needs to do so, and is not a Christian. But this man is as "religious" as the pastor at my local church.

Men and women are religious because they were created that way. We literally cannot help but be religious. All of our thinking is based on whatever faith about facts we choose, and both this choice and the subject of the choice are manifestly religious matters.

So, as we've seen, our faith about facts is our set of religious presuppositions. And these religious presuppositions are the ground of thought rather than the product of thought.[9] In this way, religious presuppositions form the building blocks of each person's worldview, and these worldviews collectively comprise the philosophy of a given culture. Each culture, then, is a product of its philosophy, and its philosophy is an expression of its religious presuppositions.[10] Religion is *not* just another manifestation of culture, as it is typically described by social scientists. Religious views are the *source* of culture. Or put another way, culture is "religion externalized."[11] In other words, cultures, like people, are inescapably religious. That's why it is silly, and at times dangerous, for political leaders to talk about social movements, terrorists, local cultures, wars, and even nation-states as not religious. Religion is germane to every discussion.

Just as each culture is the product of many people's worldviews, the spirit of an age is the product of the cultural expressions of that given period of time (a few years, a decade, a century, an epoch, and so on). This spirit of the age, or zeitgeist as it is sometimes called, is rooted in religion, or more specifically, religious presuppositions.

All thinking or reasoning is therefore circular. It begins with certain presuppositions and it arrives at conclusions determined by those presuppositions. So, for example, if you do not believe in God or accountability, then a shallow, hedonistic philosophy like "Take life easy; eat, drink, and be merry" might make sense (see Luke 12:13–21). But if you believe in God, then such a philosophy makes no sense at all.

This is why political summits that bring opposing sides like Palestinians and Israelis to the discussion table usually do not produce many agreements, let alone full agreement. Both sides work with totally different and diametrically opposed presuppositions. This doesn't mean that such talks should not take place or that some mutually agreeable decisions can't be made. It does mean that political accords between equivalent parties rarely change fundamental beliefs, and political problems are likely to occur again soon.

First principles in the form of religious presuppositions are both *temporally* and *eternally* significant. What presuppositions you adopt determine your worldview and thus who you become. What worldview(s) a culture embraces influences the inescapably religious enterprises of education, the law, business and economics, government, health care, the arts and entertainment, and much more. There is no better illustration of the old cliché "Get it right the first time" than as it applies to the religious presuppositions of your worldview. If you're wrong at the point of your most basic controlling beliefs, then you'll be wrong in everything else. Your worldview and therefore your life will be a house built not on solid rock but on shifting sand (see Matt. 7:24–27).

The apostle Peter said to Christians, "You are a chosen people, a royal priesthood, a holy nation, a people belonging to God, that you may declare the praises of him who called you out of darkness into his wonderful light" (1 Peter 2:9). To act as a blessed people, Christians must be different. They must develop their Christian worldview with the ultimate goal: "So whether you eat or drink or whatever you do, do it all for the glory of God" (1 Cor. 10:31). Since Christians live in cultures awash with many worldviews, they must be aware of the apostle Paul's warning:

> . . . that no one may deceive you by fine-sounding arguments. . . . See to it that no one takes you captive through hollow and deceptive philosophy, which depends on human traditions and the basic principles of this world rather than on Christ.
>
> Colossians 2:4, 8

> He is before all things, and in him all things hold together. . . . For God was pleased to have all his fullness dwell in him, and through him to reconcile to himself all things, whether things on earth or things in heaven.
>
> Colossians 1:17, 19

Only a truly Christian worldview fully explains reality. A Christian worldview is *big;* it's a *world*view. Only a Christian worldview allows us to worship God in spirit and in truth (see John 4:24), because a Christian worldview is the only true worldview.

CHARACTERISTICS OF A CHRISTIAN WORLDVIEW

A Christian worldview provides meaning in an otherwise unstructured and potentially meaningless world. A Christian worldview is theistically focused, biblically grounded, thoroughly and self-consciously Christian, and coherent and comprehensive.[12] No other worldview better explains the nature of reality, better provides an explanation of the source of life and who we are as human beings and as individuals, better details the source and nature of evil, or offers a better remedy for brokenness in the human condition than does a Christian worldview.

Theistically Focused

A Christian worldview is theistically focused (see 1 Cor. 3:11). Jean-Paul Sartre said that a finite point has no meaning unless it has an infinite reference point.[13] He was correct. The infinite reference and integration point of a Christian worldview is the ontological, triune, sovereign God of the universe. His self-disclosure is the ultimate basis of meaning in both his *general revelation* in a real universe and in the human heart and in *special revelation* through his Son Jesus Christ and his Word, the Bible.[14] As Francis A. Schaeffer put it, we worship "the God who is there" and "he is there and he is not silent."[15] God is truth, and he is eternal and immutable. Thus truth is possible; truth exists. Truth is what God says it is in his Word. Or another way of putting it, truth is what coheres with God's Word.

The attributes and character of the creator God endues the universe with reality and rationality. The universe is reasonable and actual. It is "there," and it may be known because God is there and in his self-disclosure has made himself known. Creator God invests meaning and intelligent design in the created order, making knowledge and science possible. His Spirit governs the universe with his *common grace,* promoting righteousness and restraining evil.[16]

God is infinite yet personal. He is the key to meaning and truth in creation, life, culture, and history. Knowing God is the ultimate spiritual endeavor, for knowing God is the basis for reconciling our own nature in a relationship with him, glorifying him, and then developing an understanding of a God-ordained creation.

In the Christian view, human beings are *imago Dei* (the image of God), beautiful and full of worth in God's eyes. Man and woman were created in a specific and unique manner, endowed with unique personality, volition, emotion, reason, and rationality by a personal God. But man and woman are morally fallen. They are fallen in sin and are in need of individual redemption. All creation is good but is now cursed as the result of human sin. To restore fellowship with the holy God, man and woman must be morally regenerated through redemption in Jesus Christ. Consequently, the Lord and Savior Jesus

Christ, not human beings, is the focus of a truly Christian worldview. "For in him we live and move and have our being" (Acts 17:28). Since the triune God is both the One and the many, the great I AM, he ultimately unifies all particulars, all data, all knowledge, all parts of the human experience and the universe. Bruce Little writes, "Since God is both the center and circumference of life and all that is, everything only has true meaning as it relates to him, the absolute universal."[17] In life, education, and science a unified field of knowledge is possible only via a Christian worldview.

Biblically Grounded

A Christian worldview is not Christian unless it is biblically grounded. A truly Christian worldview respects God's special revelation, the Bible, and therefore seeks to ground all worldview assumptions in its teachings. As God's infallible and inspired Word, the Bible is considered an objectively defined body of truth, as temporally applicable as it is eternally significant. The Bible is truth yet does not contain exhaustive truth.[18] We can and must study the created world, learning from God's *general revelation.* But we will know the world fully only as God's *special revelation,* the Bible, is known.

John Calvin noted that the Scripture interprets creation, which is necessary because of sin. Only in Scripture can we learn about the source and remedy for sin and only in Scripture do we learn who God is, why he created the world, and who we are in relationship to him. Learning can and must take place *beyond* the Scripture but is incomplete if it takes place *aside from* the Scripture. Thus understanding the Bible is an essential step in forming and applying a Christian worldview.

A biblically grounded Christian worldview begins in the Book of Genesis and roots our thinking in a knowledge of creation, thus answering the question of who we are and from whence we have come. It explains the fall of the human race into sin and the evil this perpetuates in the heart of each individual separated from God. And the Bible shares the gospel, the glorious story of redemption for human beings and all of creation through the reconciling sacrifice and resurrection of the Son of God, Jesus Christ. Consequently, a Christian worldview recognizes a remedy for sin and understands good and evil, mercy and justice, accountability and forgiveness.

Thoroughly and Self-Consciously Christian

A Christian worldview is thoroughly and self-consciously Christian. It is distinct from all non-Christian worldviews. A Christian worldview acknowledges God as supreme and his glory as ultimate, and it values God's will and pleasure above all other considerations. A Christian worldview seeks to bring every thought into captivity and to think God's thoughts after him (see 2 Cor. 10:5). Spiritual discernment as a form of Christian critical thinking forms the Spirit-driven character of a thoroughly and self-consciously Christian worldview (see Phil. 1:9–11), even as the doctrine of Christian liberty defines its expression of freedom in Christ (see Romans 14; Gal. 5:1).

A Christian worldview expresses hope regarding the nature of reality and history. It observes that history has a goal planned by God but also notes that wheat and weeds will coexist until the final day (Matt. 13:24–30).

Coherent and Comprehensive

Finally, a Christian worldview is both coherent and comprehensive. It is coherent because of its capacity to interrelate all questions without inconsistency or contradiction. It is comprehensive in that it addresses all pertinent questions, for "his divine power has given us everything we need for life and godliness through our knowledge of him" (2 Peter 1:3). In other words, a Christian worldview integrates all facts because it proclaims that all truth is created and defined by God.[19]

A Christian worldview, when applied consistently, allows Christianity to become a way of life, a thinking faith that goes beyond bumper sticker commentary and T-shirt slogans. A Christian worldview

works out ways in which biblical beliefs and values can guide constructive thought and action. It explores the relationship of Christian faith to the various areas of human learning, the findings of science in a theistic context, and valuing both scientific and artistic enterprises as God's good gifts. It brings biblical concepts of justice and love to the moral and social concerns of our times. By seeing everything in relation to the Creator-God incarnated in Jesus Christ, it gives unified meaning, direction, and hope to all we do.[20]

A Christian worldview is theistically focused, biblically grounded, thoroughly and self-consciously Christian, and coherent and comprehensive, which enables the believer to proclaim the lordship of Christ in all of life.

TWO TASKS FOR WORLDVIEW CHRISTIANS

The Christian worldview is a manner, means, and message for bringing all that we experience in culture under the scrutiny of Christian thinking in order to develop it for the glory of God. We've got work to do.

Caring for the World

First, to accomplish our task, we must understand that we have a stewardship responsibility. This is a concept that was first introduced in the Cultural Mandate (Gen. 1:28) and clearly instructs us in our caring responsibility for the world. The words *dominion* and *subdue* in the Cultural Mandate imply creative development of culture for the glory of God. This doctrine is a key statement of God's expectation that human beings will develop social and scientific enterprises. As creatures made in God's image, we're expected to offer the works of our mind and our hands to God in humble obedience and adoration.

This is the Christian's life calling,[21] a concept that was rescued from obscurity by Martin Luther and was brought to America via the writings of Puritan preacher Cotton Mather. Since the Reformation, the doctrine of a divine calling has helped Christians understand their lives as a ministry of love, service, and obedience. According to Scripture, all men and women are accorded ultimate worth and dignity before God, who in turn has a plan for each of them (see Gen. 1:26–27; Job 19:25–26; Ps. 20:4). God gives to every man and woman certain talents, and he expects them to use these talents wisely. Christians must identify those talents and seek to serve God. That's our calling. It's every Christian's calling.[22]

The specific occupation we choose in life is a matter of Christian freedom. So Christian liberal arts colleges that encourage young people to consider a wide variety of professional pursuits in their lives are actually fulfilling the Cultural Mandate. My friend who constructs and manages office buildings for a living is "about his Father's business." So is my friend who is an oncologist, using his medical knowledge to help save some people's lives while helping others understand suffering, pain, and death from a Christian perspective. My late grandfather, a farmer and carpenter who worked diligently with a desire to do things well, pleased God in his occupational choice and endeavors. One of my mentors who develops oil and gas reserves for commercial distribution is directly involved in the Cultural Mandate. My wife as a homemaker is helping to create culture, a high calling before God.

Carrying the Message

Our second task as worldview Christians is to fulfill the Great Commission (Matt. 28:19–20). The Great Commission requires that we be stewards of a message as well as a world. While we care for the world, we are to carry the message. In the Great Commission, Christ commanded that we "go and make disciples of all nations . . . teaching them to obey everything I have commanded you." Human beings are fallen, tainted from birth by sin, and thus characterized by a human predicament S. D. Gaede called our "relational dilemma" and Richard Taylor called the "Great Dislocation."[23] People are created to need the Lord, and we Christians are called to carry the message to them.

Christians know love and truth through salvation in Christ (see John 3:16). Since they have been reconciled with the Lord, the Great Commission mandates that Christians teach their beliefs, propagate truth, and further the work and proclaim the person of Jesus Christ their Lord in the world. Beliefs that are kept and not taught are soon lost to the next generation. The world needs both a literate clergy and a literate laity who implement the doctrine of the "priesthood of all believers." We do this by seeking to infuse the Christian perspective into all of life, through reading the Bible for ourselves, understanding its fullness, and then carrying the message of reconciliation to spiritually impoverished people.

I know a businessman who has led more people to Christ than anyone I have ever known. He does not accomplish this spiritual feat by passing out tracts or going door-to-door—longtime and legitimate, but sometimes ineffective, practices advocated by the evangelical community. God allows him to win souls to Christ simply through his overt enthusiasm for life in Christ, his accessible and likeable personality, and his willingness to talk to anyone about their understanding of God. His way of life invariably points people to his faith, and he's always ready to share his love for Christ. The Great Commission is for him a natural part of life.

MEN AND WOMEN OF ISSACHAR

The Christian's mission is to think distinctively and be distinctive, to be in the world but not of the world, even as we carry the message into the world. One way to accomplish this mission is to emulate the Old Testament men of Issachar. These were men "who understood the times and knew what Israel should do" (1 Chron. 12:32). They're good examples of how to apply what we're now calling a Christian worldview.

Among all the mighty men of valor, listed in this passage in 1 Chronicles, that God provided for King David in his quest to politically and spiritually solidify the nation of Israel, God sent men who knew God's commands, knew their own culture, and therefore knew what Israel ought to do. Among all the men who were experienced in the technologies of war, God sent to David men who knew how to fight but who also were spiritually and culturally aware. These men were not ignorant of God's law, they were not ignorant of the challenge of their times, so they were not ignorant of the kind of steps they should take for God's purposes, blessing, and glory.

This is the challenge of this present age. Christians must understand the Word of God. A Christian ignorant of biblical doctrine must certainly be an encouragement to the Evil One. While there is much talk today of growing biblical illiteracy, the problem and the need are deeper than this. While some Christians do not know the Bible's teachings, many other Christians know biblical stories and verses but do not know how to apply the truths taught in the Bible to everyday life—that is, many Christians do not have a developed Christian worldview.

Biblical principles are the very Word of God. It is only by the power of the Word of God as directed by the Spirit of God that Christians can hope to challenge sinful worldviews. Knowing Scripture is to know truth (Ps. 119:160; John 14:6). Christians are enjoined to know truth and to make it known. Speaking the truth in love to a culture that is morally adrift is the greatest opportunity of these times (Eph. 4:15).

Christians must understand the times. We must know the enemy and the enemy's many tactics. We must identify, learn, and critique the presuppositions of counterfeit worldviews that offer themselves as surrogates for biblical Christianity yet leave people enslaved to fate or fantasy. We must know and understand the rhythms and directions of both the spirit of this age and the inclinations of our neighbor's heart so that we can respond boldly but winsomely in God's name. And we must know the good and positive opportunities offered us in our time, learning to celebrate these gifts of God for his glory and for the benefit of our neighbors.

Contemporary men and women of Issachar are Christ-committed, biblically knowledgeable, and culturally aware Christian people. They are proactive stewards of both the Word and the world. Until Christ returns for his people, or until they pass from this earth, they know there will be spiritual battles to fight. But the Christian worldview both prepares them for and protects them in these battles so that they move confidently forward, knowing that the truth of the Lord endures forever (Ps. 117:2 KJV), and it is the truth that sets them free (John 8:32).

We know who we are. We're would-be contemporary men and women of Issachar. We know what we believe—an all-encompassing Christian worldview. But the world is changing. Do we know what we believe about social change?

3

CHRISTIAN VIEWS OF SOCIAL CHANGE

There is a time for everything, and a season for every activity under heaven.

Ecclesiastes 3:1

If indeed a Christian worldview applies to all of life, then it must address social change. Actually, God has a lot to say in his Word about both change and order. We find the beginning of the story several thousand years ago.

King Solomon was on the throne in Israel. Though he was the wisest man who ever lived, he was struggling, as Colson and Pearcey put it, with the fact that "in every human being is a deep, ongoing search for meaning and transcendence—part of the image of God in our very nature." Solomon wrestled with the notion that "even if we flee God, the religious imprint remains. Everyone believes in some kind of deity—even if that deity is an impersonal substance, such as matter, energy, or nature."[1]

To learn, to test the viability and veracity of his faith, and to seek his own validation, Solomon systematically examined the meaning of the world and life. His observations, recorded for us in Ecclesiastes, provide fundamental insights into the character of God and human beings and the dynamics of history. More than that, they help us understand how it is possible to live a fleetingly short life in a rapidly changing world yet experience significance and know that we are ultimately significant.

Solomon began his analysis by noting that death comes to everyone, making the activities of life, however noteworthy or exemplary, appear vain or meaningless. He initially finds no purpose readily identifiable in the cycles of nature or in the seemingly senseless train of events we call life (Eccles. 1:4–11).[2]

Solomon used his exalted royal position, great riches, and outstanding intellect to engage in quests to comprehend and overcome the vicissitudes of life. One by one he pursued and tested worldly wisdom, pleasure, wealth, materialism, and labor, concluding that they were "utterly meaningless! Everything is meaningless" (1:2). To Solomon it seemed that human beings are no better than animals, for one dies just like the other. All come from dust and to dust they all return (3:18–21).

Nothing the world had to offer seemed to remove the meaninglessness of the human condition. Life appeared to be an existential absurdity. Solomon recognized the futility of his study: "No one can comprehend what goes on under the sun. Despite all his efforts to search it out, man cannot discover its meaning. Even if a wise man claims he knows, he cannot really comprehend it" (8:17). With all his worldly advantages, Solomon still knew what it meant to be hopeless and despairing, and he saw emptiness looming as the only product of our fleeting existence.

But the beauty of Ecclesiastes, and more broadly the whole biblical Christian faith, is that the story of humanity doesn't end there. Although Solomon first considered life unpredictable and full of unresolvable paradoxes, he gradually acknowledged and affirmed the sovereign plan and purpose of the eternal self-existent God: "Now all has been heard; here is the conclusion of the matter: Fear God and keep his commandments, for this is the whole duty of man. For God will bring every deed into judgment, including every hidden thing, whether it is good or evil" (12:13–14). In the end, Solomon understood that "meaningfulness is a question of premises," and thus *meaning* for the creature is established in relationship to our Creator.[3]

Knowing God, the title of J. I. Packer's well-known book, expresses it well. In this book Packer explains that knowing God is the ultimate spiritual endeavor, for knowing God is the basis for glorifying him and developing an understanding of a God-ordained created order.[4] Knowing God is the beginning point for our Christian understanding of social change.

AUGUSTINE'S VIEW OF SOCIAL CHANGE

Early in the fifth century A.D., Augustine of Hippo, perhaps one of the most influential thinkers in the history of Christianity, recognized that knowing God is the essential beginning of a proper understanding of a changing world. His thinking, which focused on the sovereignty of God, has heavily influenced Christian philosophers of history and social change since that time. Augustine believed that

- creation evidences the plan or design of God;
- God never deviates from this plan;
- God's plan is gradually fulfilling itself by actualizing what was potential in creation;
- a gradual progression of knowledge, material culture, and the arts is apparent in civilization;
- man develops through stages or epochs;
- conflict is evident throughout history between the good, "City of God," and the evil, "City of Man";
- history is now in a period of decline leading to destruction.[5]

It's clear that Augustine contributed greatly to a Christian understanding of social change. He acknowledged that the ultimate and first cause is the God who preceded the cosmos, that God's will shall be accomplished in the world system, that opposing supernatural forces, which Augustine called "cities," are at work whether or not humanity is always able to detect them, and that history has a divine purpose. Like Solomon, Augustine affirmed that an infinite-personal God *is* and that he is essential to human existence.

Virtually all of these assumptions have in one way or another been rejected by predominant contemporary worldviews. Most important, currently accepted theories of social change, heavily immersed in naturalism, nearly all assume a "closed system"—a kind of natural order in which there is not, nor can there be, any contact with a supreme being (if one exists). Everything that can be known must be determined empirically, verified by one's senses. Anything that cannot be experienced by one's senses is by definition "non-sense" or nonsense.[6]

Most contemporary social theorists and many other leading academicians have simply chosen as a matter of secular faith to believe that God does not exist. And as a corollary belief, many choose to think of human beings as either active, unhindered creators (a denial of the transcendent) or passive and therefore meaningless pawns (a denial of humanity). Either way, humanity is just a cog in nature's God-free machinery.

Despite its many virtues, Augustine's conception of social change is incomplete. It leaves little room for human beings as active social agents capable of changing social history. Augustine pictures the world as a tightly ordered place with God in control. In his view human beings don't make history. With this idea Augustine influenced the medieval premise that society was an organic whole wherein human beings are expected only to seek salvation and not build culture.

Augustine also unwittingly reinforced the idea of progress.[7] His belief that human beings develop through stages and realize a gradual progression of knowledge, material culture, and the arts leaves the impression that some superior culture may someday be attained. Some non-Christian interpretations have added virtue or human morality to his list. These utopian theories assume that the human race will progress morally and that this will inevitably lead to the salvation of society. Modern culture has been highly influenced by such views, but, as we will see later, postmodern attitudes are much more pessimistic.

Augustine did not pay much attention to order or to the individual Christian's responsibility in the midst of change. So his conclusions, though insightful, influential, and helpful, do not meet all of our needs. For our rapidly changing times, we require a fuller understanding of God's world and of the Christian's role in it.

Understanding Our Role in the World

We'll organize our consideration around these questions:

1. What does God reveal about himself in the Bible?
2. What does the Bible say about the nature of human beings?

3. What does the Bible say about order?
4. What does the Bible say about change?
5. What does the Bible say causes change?
6. Does the Bible demonstrate that change has a direction?

God Reveals Himself in the Bible

Any Christian approach to the study of social change must logically begin with the nature of God. While some of these observations, along with some to follow about the nature of human beings, have already been made in the previous chapter, they are so important to our study of social change and the flow of this analysis that I'm repeating them here. Once we understand who the self-disclosed, sovereign God is and our relationship with him, we'll understand much about social change.

The Bible reveals that God exists, declaring that the man or woman who says there is no God is a fool (Ps. 14:1; 53:1). God is the external, first, and ultimate cause (Gen. 1:1; John 1:1–3). He therefore transcends time, culture, and the environment, and though he created them and works in them, he stands above yet is involved in history, society, and the cosmos. God's Word, or will, is sovereign and is "certain, secret, exhaustive, and perfect"[8] (Prov. 21:1; Eccles. 3:1–8; Dan. 4:35; Rom. 11:33–36; Rev. 4:11). God's will is a mystery (Eccles. 3:11; 7:13–14; 8:17; Dan. 3:17–18). Solomon observed that though human beings may aspire to know fully God's plan for the ages, they will not be successful. God is a God of order, and the creation he established is also good and orderly (Genesis 1).

God created the universe and all things within it (Genesis 1–2). Creation and humanity are tainted by humanity's fall into sin and groan in expectation of redemption and restoration (Genesis 3; Rom. 1:18–32; 5:12; 8:19–22). God, through his Son Jesus Christ, will *redeem* those who accept Christ as Savior and Lord and then *reconcile* all things to himself, *restoring* individuals and creation to the glory God intended for them (John 3:36; Rom. 5:18–19; 10:9–13; Col. 1:15–20). God's plan for humanity and history is evident in creation, the fall, redemption, reconciliation, and restoration, and these elements form the essential basis of a Christian worldview understanding of social change.

God *is* love (1 John 4:16), and God *is* truth (John 14:6). In these and in all of God's other attributes, he is immutable (Exod. 3:14; Ps. 102:25–27; 90:2; Isa. 40:8). God said, "I the LORD do not change" (Mal. 3:6), and in the New Testament our Lord is described: "Jesus Christ is the same yesterday and today and forever" (Heb. 13:8). He is the great I AM (Exod. 3:14; John 8:58), "the Alpha and the Omega, the First and the Last, the Beginning and the End" (Rev. 22:13). He is the infinite, objective reference point for all of creation.

God is the basis for all meaning. He is Creator and Sustainer, infinite and personal, almighty Judge and heavenly Father (Col. 1:17). "In him we live and move and have our being" (Acts 17:28).

The Nature of Human Beings

God created human beings in his image (Gen. 1:26–27). As *imago Dei,* men and women have continuity with nature and the environment, but there is also discontinuity; they are made of dust and yet uniquely created with God's breath of life (Ps. 8:3, 5). Men and women therefore have volition, emotion, rationality, and unique personality. By God's design they have significance. Human beings are active and creative social agents, capable of influencing the world in which we live through free choices but also open to being influenced by the world (Gen. 1:28).

Moreover, some decisions may be made at a socially or culturally determined subconscious level. Socialization (the process by which we adopt the behavior patterns of our surrounding culture) may determine behavior when only very limited conscious, individual will is involved. But even when socialization is properly understood and accounted for, human beings still possess the divinely appointed ability to override cultural and historical influences. We're able to make decisions that may stimulate change and that are generated by a source other than social forces.

We are not simply products of our environment or any other material or impersonal source. "A man's decisions constitute a real cause that produce an effect for which he is held accountable. He is not the ultimate cause; God is. But the man produces real secondary causes with his decisions and actions."[9]

Human beings, created by God, are good and have value and dignity surpassing all else in creation. But we have a moral problem. We are fallen, are born with a sinful nature, and consequently will die (Genesis 3; Jer. 17:9; Rom. 5:12). Human beings possess a derived or attained evil as a result of the fall and therefore require spiritual and moral regeneration. The Christian doctrines of creation and the fall account for good and evil better than all other belief systems. The fall also explains sin and death's presence in the world as destructive and disintegrative personal and social forces capable of ruining all that they touch.

As we have seen in the Book of Ecclesiastes, life is unpredictable and full of paradoxes that cannot be solved even by the "prepared" (Eccles. 1:14–15; 9:11–12). We are responsible, however, for how we use our time (Eph. 5:15–16) and are instructed in this both in the Cultural Mandate (Gen. 1:28) and the principles of stewardship (see Matt. 25:14–30; Luke 16:1–13; 19:11–27; 1 Cor. 4:4). Human beings are accountable before God for wise and faithful stewardship of all of God's gifts, those that come through creation and those that come as a result of God's redemption (Eccles. 12:13–14). The purpose of life is to glorify God (1 Cor. 10:31).

What the Bible Says about Order

God is a God of order (1 Cor. 14:33, 40) and has established order in the so-called natural laws of the universe, the seasons, and the cycles of nature (Gen. 8:22; Ps. 104:19; Eccles. 1:5–7; Rom. 8:20–22). Order, sometimes called stability or continuity, is expected to be in the individual Christian's life (Heb. 10:23). A desire for order is evident in God's ordination (i.e., ordering) of the fundamental institutions of society—the family, civil government, and the church (Genesis 2; Acts 2:42–47; Rom. 13:1–7). God's own unchanging character communicates structure *(stasis)* to all that he has created (Mal. 3:6; Heb. 13:8). In the Old and New Testament principles of human relationships, order is apparent. God's sovereign will, defined in Scripture and developed in history, is a picture of order, for it portrays an all-encompassing master plan that God worked out in detail before the foundation of the world (Eph. 1:4, 11; Revelation 1–22).

What the Bible Says about Change

Change exists. It is evident in Scripture, Old to New Testament, law to grace, Israel to the church. Salvation in the life of the individual is a revolutionary change. Social change leading to a markedly different history may result from divine intervention (see Genesis 11) or from satanic intervention allowed by God (Job 1–3; Eph. 2:2). Satan is described as the "ruler of the kingdom of the air," and like the heavenly Father, Satan also has a plan for history.

The parable of the wheat and the weeds teaches that both God and Satan, good and evil, have a plan for the world, and no amount of Christian determination will eradicate evil until God intervenes at the end of earthly time (Matt. 13:24–30, 36–43). Prophecy predicts future change and the fulfillment of God's redemptive work through Christ in history (Daniel 7–12; Revelation 1–22).

Planned change is also evident in Scripture. Human beings may plan but are to do so in God's will and without arrogance (James 4:13–15). Planned change is the goal of individual sanctification (Romans 6–8), and spiritual development should be an ongoing process in the life of every believer.

What the Bible Says Causes Change

Social change occurs for at least seven reasons:

1. The inscrutable purposes of God (Gen. 1:1; 11; Eccles. 3:11; 7:13–14; 9:11; Dan. 3:17–18; John 1:1–3).
2. Christ's redemptive work in history (John 3:16; 1 Corinthians 15; Col. 1:15–19; 1 Thess. 4:14–18; Revelation 1–22).
3. The conscious, creative, and active efforts of men and women or humanity (Gen. 1:27–28; 2:15; 1 Cor. 10:31).
4. The destructive results of the fall or the curse, including the death of individual men and women (Genesis 3; Rom. 5:12; 8:18–20; Heb. 9:27).
5. Satanic or demonic intervention (Job 1–3; Eph. 2:2).
6. Unintended or unanticipated change as an indirect or direct result of the actions of finite human beings in what for them is an uncertain environment (Eccles. 1:14–15; 9:1–12).
7. Social forces that can and often do transcend individual human beings or society (Matt. 13:24–30, 36–43).

God may intervene in history as a response to prayer or for his own purposes, wholly unknown to man. Likewise, the exercise of human volition and the action that follows it may cause social change. Society begins as a creation of God and humanity and gradually becomes an objective reality in itself. Then, in turn, society influences human beings via socialization.[10] Society may influence itself to change through a process known as implosion and may contribute to change in other societies via diffusion, acculturation, or conquest. Thus social change may be partially due to an ongoing dialectic between humanity and society and between God and humanity—all within the context of God's will.

While many contemporary worldviews consider humanity simply an element in a cosmic machine, the Christian position rather obviously rejects all forms of closed system determinism. There is no closed system, for God is the creator of the universe, and he continues his involvement in it. There is no determinism, for human beings are given the ability to choose. The Christian worldview properly considers God the originator and director of the system and casts humanity in a potentially (and responsibly) innovative role. Garry Friesen's work on decision making helps us visualize the relationship of human beings to God's will:

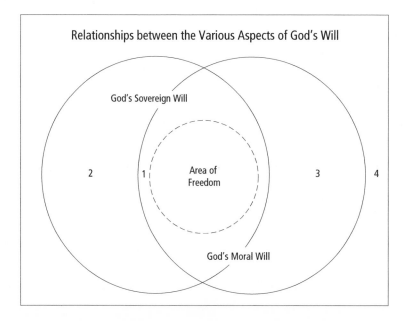

Friesen describes each part of the illustration as

1. Acts done in fulfillment both of God's sovereign will and his moral will (Scripture).
2. Acts outside God's moral will yet fulfilling his sovereign will, i.e. the Crucifixion.
3. Acts within God's moral will but not within his sovereign will. These will never occur but are included to illustrate God's omniscience.
4. Any potential sinful act that does not come to pass.[11]

Any attempt to portray God's sovereign control of the universe in diagrammatic form inevitably suffers from oversimplification. But Friesen does portray the essence of the most profound of Christian beliefs: God actively controls (meaning sovereignty, not determinism) time, history, and both individual and social change. Men and women freely operate within the parameters of this divine governance.

The Direction of Change

Scripture clearly indicates that history, and therefore social change within it, has directionality. God is moving history (His-story) to a fruition that men and women can only minimally comprehend based on God's revelation in Scripture.

A Christian view of social change must rest on an understanding of the infinite-personal God and a created humanity. Both God and human beings have divinely ordained places in the created order. Human beings are responsible before God for their actions in this changing universe.

As we noted earlier, in some secularized versions of social history, human beings are painted as helpless pawns whose actions are determined by social forces and who are left to wander pessimistically through their days on earth with little hope of a more significant existence. In some other secularized versions, too much independence is assigned human reason and technique, resulting in science or knowledge being considered the savior of humanity. A transcendent God is of no more concern in these interpretations than voodoo.

But in Christian thought, history is teleological, meaning it has a goal. The biblical story is the record of God's redemptive work and sin's ruinous leaven in human history. This history features constructive good and destructive evil, hope and despair, joy and anguish. Social history simultaneously reveals progress, regress, and decline. Humanity's ability to ascertain the difference between progress, regress, and decline is at best limited.

Various theological views of future things, the study of *eschatology*, interpret social change, history, and the possibility of progress in quite different ways. *Historic* and *dispensational premillennialism* tend to view the future rather pessimistically, citing many passages of Scripture that speak of the last days as characterized by rampant moral decline (Romans 1; 1 Thessalonians 4; 2 Thessalonians 2; 2 Timothy 3). Premillennialism generally describes the direction of change in terms of decline or deterioration, a steady descent from the Garden of Eden. While premillennialism is very optimistic about the possibility of individual change through conversion to Christianity (regeneration or being born again), many who embrace premillennialism are less sanguine about the possibility of real and lasting change in society.

Postmillennialism and *amillennialism* tend to be somewhat more optimistic about the possibility of spiritually appropriate societal and cultural change in history. Though these interpretations recognize moral decay, they tend to emphasize the victory of Christ over sin and Satan and focus their efforts on reclaiming a fallen world to prepare for Christ's coming (1 Cor. 13:9–13).

We must admit that our limited knowledge is apparent in all eschatological teachings. The Bible unquestionably posits a goal for social history, but determining whether society, or more likely multiple societies with complex characteristics, will progress, decline, or regress is still problematic.

American Christian historian E. H. Harbison noted that the problem is how to see history "as governed by a predestinating Providence without falling into the sin of playing God."[12] Christians must carefully test their ideas of the directionality of social change or history against the Bible. One thing is clear. No naturalistic utopia based on a faith in humanity, science, or education will ever occur nor is such a goal tenable for anyone maintaining a biblically rooted theology.

Progress—material, technological, artistic, political, or scientific— may occur under the province of the doctrine of common grace. Humanity's knowledge does accumulate. Unregenerate men and women are still made in God's image and possess God-given abilities to develop knowledge. But human beings cannot improve their culture morally without the regenerative work of the Holy Spirit or the impact of the Christian ethos in society.

It seems to me that our analysis of what the Scripture says about change and order leads us, among other things, to be wary of equating progress with success or prosperity with God's blessing. It is quite possible that the development we experience, like the events described in the biblical books of Hosea, Amos, and Malachi, is rooted in a source other than Christian effort or divine sanction. A Christian view of progress is built on the fact that God works all things together for good to those who love God and are called according to his purpose. This is true in terms of our responsibility as stewards to develop culture, our faith in the Spirit's regenerative and restorative power, and our hope anticipating God's perfect resolution of history (Rom. 8:28).

A CHRISTIAN VIEW OF SOCIAL CHANGE

In summary, a Christian view of social change involves all of the following components:

- God exists and is the eternal, first, and ultimate cause.
- God transcends time, cultures, and the environment, ontologically standing above yet involved in governing history, society, and the cosmos.
- God is enacting an exhaustive plan for the ages that is only partially revealed in the Bible. Scripture focuses primarily on the redemptive work of Christ in history.
- God is a God of order and that which he created is orderly.
- God's character does not change, but he values both change and order.
- Men and women are created in God's image with volition, emotion, rationality, and unique personality.
- Men and women are active and creative social agents, though they are often socialized into societal and cultural patterns of behavior.
- Men and women are morally destitute and in a fallen condition before God. Fellowship with God has been broken and must be reconciled. This is the essential problem. All other problems are

derivatives of this one. Men and women must therefore experience moral regeneration through Christ to achieve salvation.

- Sin, as a result of the fall, is a destructive and disintegrative force in nature and in social history. Death, the consequence of sin, terminates the existence of men and women on earth and therefore also introduces change.
- Change exists and may be planned or unplanned.
- Change may result from divine, satanic, or human intervention; social interaction; or social forces.
- Both good and evil exist contemporaneously in social history, leading to progress and regress, improvement and decline.

With our biblical background thus far, we ought to be able to begin to discern certain Christian and non-Christian themes in these changing times. These themes should increase our understanding of the world and help us know how to relate properly to it.

If we discover that change is best understood when we learn God's definitions, God's principles, and God's commands, then we'll be able to interact Christianly with change of any kind. That spells not only a lessening of fear but, better yet, joy and spiritually productive culture-building that honors God.

More important, we understand that redemption in Jesus Christ means restoration of an original good creation. You and I are called to promote renewal or reformation in all of God's creation. This certainly includes, but does not stop with, leading people to regeneration in Christ. If Christ is the reconciler of all things (Col. 1:20) and we are ministers of reconciliation (2 Cor. 5:18), then we have a redemptive assignment wherever our vocation places us in the world. Redemption, restoration, regeneration, renewal, reformation, and reconciliation all entail change.

God expects us not only to handle change well but to create or produce God-honoring change. "Biblical religion is historically progressive, not reactionary. It views the whole course of history as a movement from a garden to a city, and it fundamentally affirms the movement."[13]

Christians with a fully developed, biblically Christian worldview are God's change agents. Our responsibility and privilege is to develop the spiritual discernment necessary for learning what should and what should not be changed.

4

SPIRITUAL DISCERNMENT

Christian Critical Thinking

My son, preserve sound judgment and discernment, do not let them
out of your sight; they will be life for you, an ornament to grace your
neck.

Proverbs 3:21–22

I remember watching *Home Improvement* with my boys when they
were very young. Tim "The Tool Man" Taylor and his show
were hilarious, and for the most part I thought the show represented some of the better comedy on television (until later when
Tim's boys on the show entered their teenage years and programs
began dealing with topics pertaining to adolescent sexuality).

But one ongoing characteristic of *Home Improvement* particularly
annoyed me. The boys lied to their parents constantly and were sel-
dom held accountable for it. Even worse, in later programs, Tim
began lying periodically to his wife, Jill, and she lied a few times to
him—even about whom they had been with and where they had
been. Most of the lies were literally laughed off. Only very rarely did
anyone say, "I'm sorry," and no one ever talked about right and wrong.

Regular, undisciplined lying as a part of family life in the *Home
Improvement* program was significantly different from the family life

71

portrayed on *The Cosby Show* a decade earlier. The kids lied to their parents in that program too, but never without eventually receiving a serious comeuppance from Mother or Dad or usually both parents. Lying in Dr. and Mrs. Huxtable's household was a clearly designated wrong, harmful to the child and the family. Lying in the Taylor household was a laughable means to an end.

When I began hearing the Taylor boys lying, I'd say to my three sons, "Did you hear that? He just lied to his dad. That's wrong." They'd nod and say, "Sure." But a few weeks later, my boys started beating me to the punch, energetically observing, "Dad, did you hear that? He lied. He lied to his dad." In their young hearts and minds my boys were learning a powerful lesson in spiritual discernment—they were beginning to distinguish right from wrong in their culture.

The Christian Missing Link

In order to live our lives with a consistently and thoroughly Christian worldview, we must learn "to apply unchanging biblical principles in a rapidly changing world."[1] We must learn to live with, interact with, respond to, and create change. Why? Because, as we saw in the last chapter, our unchanging sovereign Lord is in charge of change, and he commands us to be involved in change that will bring reconciliation to a sin-tainted world.

In this chapter, I want to deal more specifically with the fact that change tends to challenge old values, and a loosening of old values puts pressure on the interpreters of Christianity as well as on those of any other historic belief.[2] New social circumstances call for a new application of Christian faith. Yet too often Christians opt for what seems to be the safer approach of simply repeating rules of behavior they learned in their youth. Consequently, Christians lose an opportunity to influence social change at its inception.

This is the opportunity represented by today's youth, soon to be the twenty-first century's first young adults. Telling them not to dance is one thing; telling them *why* you believe they shouldn't dance (if this is your belief) is something else. Telling young people not to pierce their bodies is one thing (if this is your belief); telling them *why* is another challenge altogether. Try explaining to them why some church youth groups schedule dances and others consider this activity a sin. The old arguments don't work. Simple appeals to authority—"Our church has always done it this way"—don't work with this generation.

Our spiritual challenge and opportunity is to match or apply unchanging biblical truth to the needs of the changing culture. To do this we must understand biblical teachings, our Christian worldview, and our changing culture.

In the Old Testament Book of Hosea, God lamented that his people were "destroyed from lack of knowledge" (4:6). In the New Testament, Paul said, "Do not conform any longer *to the pattern of this world,* but *be transformed by the renewing of your mind.* Then you will be able to test and approve what God's will is—his good, pleasing and perfect will" (Rom. 12:2, italics mine). While many Christians possess spiritual strength of heart and soul, they are woefully undeveloped in the strength of their mind.[3] Too often, because of our lack of knowledge, we are seduced and sometimes destroyed by human philosophies.

For Christians to respond to and reform culture, we must understand the patterns of this world. Then we must avoid conforming to its ungodly elements through the transformation that comes in the renewing of our minds. This transformation produces discernment, giving us the ability to know what is ungodly. God says, "Be very careful, then, how you live—not as unwise but as wise, making the most of every opportunity, because the days are evil" (Eph. 5:15–16). The key to effectiveness in this divine-human endeavor of reforming culture is spiritual discernment, an essential part of our Christian worldview.

Discernment is a special type of spiritual insight, something God expects every Christian to develop with the help of the Holy Spirit. God commands us to "preserve sound judgment and discernment, do not let them out of your sight" (Prov. 3:21). Discernment is a spiritual capacity, the ability to see life for what it really is. It is Christian critical thinking. The apostle Paul uses several Greek terms for discernment, which denote "judging" or "testing." Discernment is "that habit of faith by which we are properly disposed to hear God's Word, and properly disposed to respond to that Word in the practical circumstances of our lives."[4] Spiritual discernment, developed within us by the Holy Spirit, enables us to differentiate, to distinguish, and to clearly define fact from fiction and truth from error in the world around us (Ps. 119:99–100, 125; Heb. 5:12–14). By God's grace, our Christian character and our ability to discern grow through learning God's Word and experiencing moral choices in life.

Spiritual discernment might be considered the Christian missing link. It's missing in that all too often people seem not to use it in their decision making. Spiritual discernment is the link between knowledge of the Word of God and the application of this knowledge to our cultural experience. On the one hand Christians read and interact with Scripture, and on the other hand they confront culture; yet too often these two activities never connect. It's another form of the sacred/secular dichotomy, a sort of Christian schizophrenia that we act out in our everyday lives. For would-be "men and women of Issachar," it doesn't work.

On the typical Christian college campus and in the average evangelical church, for example, it's fairly easy to find people who can quote verse after verse of Scripture or who can relate many Bible stories. Yet many of them cannot offer any comment at all on what those verses mean for our life today or what relevance a story like Daniel in the lion's den holds for practical living. They possess biblical knowledge. They would not fail a biblical literacy test. They may not know theology, but they aren't biblical ignoramuses either. Knowing a little about *what* they believe but not *why* they believe it means that they don't possess spiritual discernment, which requires Christian critical thinking and application skills.

The story of Lot in the Book of Genesis (19:1–38) is a lesson in the dangers of cultural captivity, something that can happen to a life that is lacking spiritual discernment. Lot chose to live in Sodom. He became a successful business leader in the city, and he allowed himself to become immersed in a non-Christian culture, even to the point of thinking and, later, acting immorally. Because he did not exercise spiritual discernment, he made a series of wrong choices that led to the loss of his character, his sons-in-law, his possessions, his wife, and his daughters' morality and spiritual commitment. Lot never learned spiritual discernment.

LEARN TO DISCERN

Spiritual discernment is a form of sophisticated spiritual wisdom that is developed through time, effort, experience, and, most important, the grace of God. The world we live in is not a spiritually friendly place. Jesus said, "I am sending you out like sheep among wolves. Therefore be as shrewd as snakes and as innocent as doves" (Matt. 10:16). We need spiritual discernment (sometimes referred to as "discretion") for spiritual protection as well as productivity: "Then you will understand what is right and just and fair—every good path. For wisdom will enter your heart, and knowledge will be pleasant to your soul. Discretion will protect you, and understanding will guard you" (Prov. 2:9–11).

Spiritual discernment is rooted in God's Word, perhaps best expressed in Paul's letter to the Philippians: "And this is my prayer: that your love may abound more and more in knowledge and depth of insight, so that you may be able to discern what is best and may be pure and blameless until the day of Christ, filled with the fruit of righteousness that comes through Jesus Christ—to the glory and praise of God" (1:9–11). In this passage of Scripture, the apostle Paul tells his Christian friends at Philippi that he wants them to experience Christian love, a love based on knowledge, not love that is frivolous or uninformed. It's love that is grounded.

The Spirit of God uses Paul's desire for his Christian converts in this ancient city to tell Christians that we must develop knowledge and depth of insight to discern what is best. Knowledge comes from biblical doctrine and an understanding of and obedience to biblical orthodoxy. In the Old Testament, knowledge was rooted in "This is what the Lord says," and in the New Testament, spiritual knowledge develops from Jesus' "I tell you the truth." You cannot be a thriving, God-blessed Christian with a fully developed Christian worldview without knowing and obeying God's will expressed in biblical truth.

It's helpful to look at these Philippians verses in reverse. Ultimately, we must bring "glory and praise to God." How do we do this? By being "filled with the fruit of righteousness that comes through Jesus Christ." How is this accomplished? By being "pure and blameless until the day of Christ." And how do we live a pure and blameless life? By taking care "to discern what is best." How do we determine what is best? By employing our "depth of insight." And from where does this insight come? From "knowledge." And finally, why would we want to do this? Because God's love characterizes our lives.

Spiritual discernment must be prayerfully nurtured, for it is an act of worship and an attribute of a spiritually mature life. As such it is a key component of a thoroughly Christian worldview. The author of Hebrews tells us how important spiritual discernment is. Whoever he was, like one of our firm but favorite teachers from grade school, he may have been a bit frustrated when he said:

> We have much to say about this, but it is hard to explain because you are slow to learn. In fact, though by this time you ought to be teachers, you need someone to teach you the elementary truths of God's word all over again. You need milk, not solid food! Anyone who lives on milk, being still an infant, is not acquainted with the teaching about righteousness. But solid food is for the mature, who by constant use have trained themselves to distinguish good from evil.

Hebrews 5:11–14

What did he say? His message is that spiritual maturity is always characterized by at least two attributes: a developed understanding of the Bible's teaching about righteousness and constant application of these teachings. By applying biblical knowledge on an ongoing basis, mature believers train themselves to distinguish (spiritually discern) good from evil.

THE WORD FOR ALL TIMES, COUNTRIES, AND CULTURES

As I stressed earlier, the Bible is God's inspired moral will expressed in principle form for all people of all times in all countries from all ethnic or racial groups in all cultures. The Bible is truly transcultural and transhistorical in its reach. Since the Scripture was given, no person and no historical period ever has been or will be beyond the reach and application of God's special revelation. No social change is a surprise to God and no social change, however small or far-reaching, however global or personal, is beyond the control of God or the critique of biblical Christianity as developed by Christian people.

Since the Bible is given for all times, countries, and cultures, it should be obvious that no one time, country, culture, or person can claim that the Bible is uniquely theirs. There can be no private interpretation or ethnic, racial, or cultural theology that is different from the Word of God (Acts 17:26–28; Gal. 3:26–29; 2 Peter 1:20–21).

The Bible is God's self-revelation to the universal church, a supraethnic community of Christian love.[5]

One of the fundamental principles of a spiritually discerning Christian worldview is recognizing that God and the Bible do not change, but virtually everything else does. It's as though the Bible is written in ink and everything else is in pencil. I've made this point in innumerable ways in this text up to this point, but it bears repeating that it is enormously and eternally comforting to know that God is the immutable anchor of the universe.

Perhaps the most useful application of this principle for our developing spiritual discernment is simply the acknowledgement that "everything" means *everything*. This includes entire cultures as well as all the small things Christian people and churches spend innumerable hours and amazing levels of spiritual energy debating (decrying, fighting)—trends, fads, and fashions that are by definition transitory.

When we spiritualize cultural forms, we can become victims of cultural captivity, guilty of private interpretations or theological provincialism. We would do well to remember H. R. Inge's statement: "He who marries the spirit of an age soon finds himself a widower."[6] However, without some cultural forms becoming traditions, life would become nearly impossible, because tradition is memory. The spiritual discernment challenge for our Christian worldview is to discern which traditions and which changes should be embraced.

RESPECT FOR TRADITION

Traditions are cultural conventions, built up over time, based on some original beliefs or intentions. Traditions are "institutionalized" habits—personal or organizational. A tradition in itself is not wrong, nor is it something to be feared, for traditions can add vitality and meaning to our lives. But tradition by definition is more about continuity than change, and the existence of a given tradition may prove to be a good or a bad thing in terms of people's ability to respond well to continuing social change.

Traditions become so familiar and at times so beloved that they gradually become "invisible" parts of an individual worldview. Consequently, because traditions are so much a part of the everyday nature of our lives, they are only rarely evaluated. This fact of life is as much a characteristic of the church as it is any other group of people, religious or nonreligious. Christians develop traditions designed to put biblical mandates into practice, but they also develop traditions, perhaps even dogma, that are separate from and go beyond the specific doctrines of Scripture. Because of this tendency, Christians need to take spiritual stock of their traditions. Are they biblically defensible? Are they accomplishing the purposes for which they were created, or have they evolved over time into an end in themselves? Is this biblically justifiable?

The Old Testament is filled with references to lawfully devised Israelite practices that became useful cultural traditions. Consider just the story of Ruth and the kinsman-redeemer relationship that provided her with a husband, Boaz (Ruth 3). This cultural tradition seems strange, even questionable, to us today, but God used it to accomplish his purposes in not only Ruth and Boaz's lives but also in the historical lineage of Joseph, the husband of Jesus' mother, Mary (Matt. 1:5).

Queen Esther employed a custom or tradition to gain access to King Xerxes and save her Jewish people from slaughter (Esther 5:1–5). In the New Testament, Jesus observes all the laws and traditions of the time, of Judaism, and of his people, the Jews, that did not specifically violate the moral will of God (Matt. 5:17–20; Luke 6:1–10).

Traditions developed from beliefs based on biblical revelation are praised in Scripture (Gal. 1:12; 2 Thess. 2:15; 3:6). In 1 Corinthians 11:23–29 the purpose and principles underlying communion are presented. In a similar manner, the Pauline Epistles provide many instructions on the working patterns of the local church, which over time have been enacted in various ways as Christian traditions.

Tradition is a common, useful, and spiritually appropriate behavior of culture building. As Henry Van Til puts it: "Man has the urge (will), the calling (must), the privilege (may), but also the power (can) to execute the creative mandate of God."[7] Men and women may build culture, and part of that construction is comprised of God-honoring traditions.

CRITICISM OF TRADITION

The Bible also has something to say about bad traditions. In fact Christians are specifically warned about traditions that stem from false worldviews. This injunction is found in Colossians 2:8, in which the apostle Paul cautioned the church in Colosse to "see to it that no one takes you captive through hollow and deceptive philosophy, which depends on human tradition and the basic principles of this world rather than on Christ." The Bible criticizes traditions that get in the way of truth. A prime example of this is found in Matthew 15:1–20. In this passage the Pharisees and teachers of the law challenged Jesus. They accused his disciples of breaking the traditions of the elders by eating with unwashed hands. In Mark 7:1–23, another record of this story, the biblical author notes that the Pharisees observed many ceremonial traditions of the elders, like washing cups, pitchers, and kettles. For the Pharisees, many religiously developed traditions were sacrosanct.

Jesus responded by pointing out inconsistencies in the Pharisees' practices, saying, "You nullify the word of God for the sake of your tradition" (Matt. 15:6). Then he called them hypocrites, applying Isaiah's prophecy to them: "These people honor me with their lips, but their hearts are far from me. They worship me in vain; their teachings are but rules taught by men" (Matt. 15:8–9).

The Pharisees of Jesus' day were known not only for their adherence to the law of God but also for their interpretations of that law, which in time became their traditions. Self-righteous adherence to traditions was a hallmark of Pharisaism. The Pharisees participated in public religious acts to be seen by others (Matthew 23). Their motivation was not worship but display. Jesus judged their attitude rather than their actions, rejecting their ritualism, traditionalism, and legalism. What mattered to Jesus was not this semblance of obedience but real obedience of the heart. His teaching was like Samuel's message to King Saul: "To obey is better than sacrifice" (1 Sam. 15:22).

"Their teachings are but rules taught by men" (Matt. 15:9). This spiritually devastating pronouncement succinctly states the critical definition of a bad tradition. If the tradition is built on human beings' false philosophies, or if the tradition has displaced biblical principles and purposes, the tradition is not biblically defensible. It must be set aside.

But traditions are traditions, in part, because of their tenacity. Passed from one generation to the next, good or bad, they help define cultures and communities; and people hold to traditions like life itself. People create culture one tradition at a time, each being an extension of their religious worldview. All this emphasizes the point that the appropriateness of a tradition should be spiritually discerned.

American churches are known for traditions that at times we've tried to export along with the gospel message. For example, more than one missionary has had to stop and think about whether flowers are really necessary for the front of the church. The American flag and the Christian flag appear on most American church platforms. Some churches will pledge allegiance to the flag in the church and deem this admirable patriotism. Others avoid saying the pledge, considering this a form of national idolatry. Neither flowers nor flags can be found in Scripture, which does not make them wrong but also means they aren't required.

The practice of having meals at the church can be found in Scripture. In days gone by, Christians debated whether eating in the church facility was biblical, given what the apostle Paul said in 1 Corinthians 11:34 about eating at home. Some churches actually built fellowship halls near, but not touching, the sanctuary building. Today this argument seems moot, for most church buildings include large fellowship halls in the basement or adjoining parts of the facility.

Baptism anywhere other than in the church baptistery has at times been condemned. This perspective and practice are especially curious because Jesus' baptism took place in the Jordan River (Matt. 3:13–17). Nevertheless, some churches developed a tradition of church baptisms only. It was a bit of a shock for my wife and me as a young married couple when we first heard this view stated in a church in Cleveland, Ohio, for Sarah had been baptized as a child in the Coal River in West Virginia. I was baptized as a child in my home church in Ohio. The pastor put me under the water, pulled me partially up, then put me under again and shook me. I've never been quite sure what that meant. Either way, Sarah and I both got wet and both made a public profession of faith. God must sometimes be amused at our silly human preoccupations.

HOLY LISTS

God's Word clearly provides us with his changeless, revealed moral will. For this to be so and for the Bible to carry an eternally relevant message, the Word must be characterized by principles or propositions. These are the biblical principles and propositions to which we have now regularly referred, and they comprise what Francis A. Schaeffer called the "true truth" of the Bible.[8]

Through these principles, God provides humanity with certain *moral absolutes* that he knows are for our benefit. For example, we are to be sexually moral all of our lives, no matter what our age, no matter in what culture we find ourselves. We know this because in his Word God gives us many statements about sexual propriety and several warnings about lust (1 Cor. 6:12–20; Eph. 5:12–13; Col. 3:1–10; 2 Tim. 2:22). We are also to be always honest. These moral absolutes do not change depending on the circumstances. They are not morally neutral matters. Sexual morality and honesty are nonnegotiable, supracultural principles.

God expects Christians to be modest, no matter the cultural context. We know this because God devised clothing and gave it to Adam and Eve in the Garden (Gen. 3:21). Modesty is a nonnegotiable principle. But it's a bit different from the principles of sexual morality and honesty, for modesty can be greatly and perhaps appropriately influenced by cultural perspective. This is where Christians must exercise spiritual discernment. Determining appropriately modest clothing and behavior in a given cultural context requires mature Christian thinking. And though there are these opportunities when we must use our own discretion about our behavior, this does not alter the fact that God gives us absolute values in his Word. In fact our determination of what is right depends on those absolute values.

People tend to focus on the "don'ts" of Scripture more than the "dos." For example, God's definition of a sexually moral relationship is considered a restrictive "don't" by many people. They do not want their sexual expression to be limited to monogamous, heterosexual marriage. Yet God's emphasis in his Word is not so much on the evil and debilitating impact of sexual immorality as it is on the blessing and benefits of a godly, sexually moral relationship. In reality, God's gift to humanity is a "do," not a "don't."

Here are two more "dos," ones that classify as moral absolutes: "Love the Lord your God with all your heart and with all your soul

and with all your mind and with all your strength" and "Love your
neighbor as yourself" (Mark 12:30–31). Jesus said there are no commandments greater than these. Note that they are positive commands, not limitations. "Honor your father and mother" is another
positive "do" command (Mark 10:19; Eph. 6:2).

But what about "Do not murder" or "Do not steal" (Mark 10:19)?
These appear to be "don'ts," but are they really? Is God trying to
restrict our behavior, or are these commandments really God's affirmation of the value of life and the moral legitimacy of personal property? Both life and property are liberties, even rights, that today we
consider fundamental to the functioning of a free society.

People frequently complain that biblical Christianity is a rule-
bound worldview, but a closer look doesn't bear this out. God's holy
list of dos and don'ts is really not that long, but since it deals with
the foundational concerns of life across all cultures, we ignore these
absolute moral values at our own peril. We can be sure that God's
"don'ts" are always for our benefit.

God's "do list" includes the fruit of the Spirit, the character issues
given in Galatians 5:22–23: love, joy, peace, patience, kindness, goodness, faithfulness, gentleness, and self-control. Elsewhere in Scripture
God says to be compassionate, forgiving, truthful, humble, loving and
submissive to a spouse, obedient to parents, and just (Eph. 4:25–32;
Col. 3:12–20).

God's "don't list" also deals with character issues. In Galatians
5:19 God warns us against sexual immorality, impurity, debauch-
ery, idolatry, witchcraft, hatred, discord, jealousy, fits (and maybe
fists) of rage, selfish ambition, dissensions, factions, envy, drunk-
enness, and orgies. In Ephesians 4:25–32 and 5:1–6, God says
"Don't" to lying, anger, stealing, unwholesome talk, bitterness,
rage and anger, brawling, slander, malice, greed, obscenity, foolish
talking, and coarse joking. All in all, while there are a few more
of God's moral absolutes we could add here, it still is not that long
a list. More important, it's God's list and therefore it's what he
intended.

Creating Our Own Holy Lists

Religious people, Christians included, tend to create their own
lists of approved beliefs, behaviors, and practices. Over time these

lists become the traditions that define the boundaries of acceptability within the group. In itself, this human tendency is not necessarily a sinister or even threatening phenomenon. Indeed, it can be just the opposite, a group strengthening and integrating function essential to the survival and enjoyment of the group and its purpose. From a Christian perspective, creating our own traditions becomes spiritually negative and threatening when and only when these traditions begin to diverge, then depart altogether, from biblical principles.

Religious people who do not know Christ as their Savior begin building the temple of their lives on the shifting sands of false belief. They may build with sincerity but without a knowledge of the truth. It's sad that Christians seem just as prone as any other group of religious or even nonreligious people to develop and embrace false traditions. As believers, we've laid a foundation beginning with the Chief Cornerstone, Jesus Christ; then we all too often build our own temple with our own traditions on top. I believe a lot of these Christians (and sometimes it could be you or me) are building in sincerity but lacking an awareness of the degree to which their temple's composition is more human tradition than biblical teaching.

The first danger to a living and culturally relevant Christian faith is unbiblical traditions. Following quickly on the heels of the first, the second danger is a pronounced human tendency to begin to judge others not on the basis of the revealed Word of God but on the basis of human traditions. Now we've created our own holy list. Holy lists are just that. They are a codification of what we believe is holy: Do this and you will be holy. Or don't do this and you will be holy.

Let's hit the pause button for a moment. I'm not suggesting that it's wrong to want to be holy. God said, "Be holy, because I am holy" (Lev. 11:44–45). Nor am I suggesting that it's wrong to identify in list form what we believe God's Word teaches or what actions our beliefs demand or imply. I am saying that Christians tend to create lists of acceptable beliefs and practices—beyond that which God commands—then judge other people by their list, not just by God's commands. It's like saying, "God gave us the Ten Commandments, but I don't think that's enough. So I'm going to have Fifteen Com-

mandments—and you've got to live up to the fifteen if you expect
to be *really* holy."

If our holy list presents nothing more than biblical principles or
clearly stated doctrines that are God's expectations for his people,
then perhaps our evaluating others' spirituality is on safe ground. But
all too often—in fact usually—our holy list presents biblical principles *plus* our own traditions (or it may contain *only* our own traditions). What we're really doing then in evaluating others' spirituality is testing their beliefs and practices by our traditions, not by God's
Word. This starts a Christian culture war.

Holy Lists That Start Christian Culture Wars

Christian culture wars have long been a part of human history.
Sometimes whole nations or empires have collided in religious battles over territory, beliefs, and practices. Christians have fought
internecine conflicts over the most esoteric issues. We cannot be
proud of this history and we should not trivialize it. In the name of
Christianity, unknown numbers of people have at times been tor-
tured and killed for simply believing something a bit different from
the dominant group. The sad thing is that the persecutors often
thought they were glorifying God.

Contemporary holy wars are taking place around the globe in
places like Northern Ireland, Bosnia, and the Middle East. Power
politics and racial or ethnic hatred are evident, but all these conflicts
are rooted in religious worldviews. There isn't much holiness in holy
wars.

America has its own version of cultural warfare. And in whatever
form it takes, it's always spiritually devastating. As we saw in the first
chapter, America's cultural warfare begins with the rejection of the
idea of absolute truth—right and wrong. This is a recipe for social
disintegration. The act of believing in truth, particularly religiously
expressed truth, is a *centripetal force* in society. It binds people together
in common understanding. Rejecting the idea of absolute truth is a
centrifugal force. Everyone does what's right in his or her own eyes,
and society gradually tears apart.

A well-developed ability to spiritually discern God's truth from
mere tradition is part of a fully functioning, comprehensive Christian worldview. The greater our capacity for spiritual discernment,

the greater is our ability to separate truth from error in contemporary culture. This capacity for spiritual discernment is a result of both grace and work, and it will serve us well in cultural matters both great and small. Mature spiritual discernment is a key component of one of the great doctrines of Scripture, our Christian liberty.

5

REDISCOVERING
CHRISTIAN LIBERTY

It is for freedom that Christ has set us free. Stand firm, then, and do
not let yourselves be burdened again by a yoke of slavery.

Galatians 5:1

Christian liberty is one of those biblical doctrines that Christians want for themselves but apparently not for anyone else. Like the disciples of old, we'd rather feud with each other over who is more spiritual than fix our thoughts on Jesus and his calling. Meanwhile the world around us is caught up in one "ism" after another, and Christians have missed Martin Luther's reminder that to fight at any point except where the battle is currently raging is a waste of time.[1] One way to do something about this is to rediscover Christian liberty.

Christian liberty is a distinctive component of a fully developed Christian worldview, offering both *spiritual liberty,* freeing Christians from the servitude of sin and yokes of spiritual bondages,[2] and *practical liberty,* freeing Christians to function biblically in a culturally relevant manner.

Christian liberty allows for traditions but, when properly understood, keeps us from being shackled by them. Christian liberty allows for change but keeps us from losing our spiritual moorings. Christian liberty enables the church to enjoy both unity and diversity in the service of the Lord. Backed by spiritual discernment, Christian liberty empowers our cultural critique even as it frees Christians to build culture to the glory of God.

Christian liberty has been applied to everything from questions relating to fasting (Mark 2:18–22) to debates about whether Christians should lie to the Gestapo about the location of Jews in hiding.[3] The available debatable issues are virtually unlimited because cultural innovation is virtually unlimited, based on human beings' God-given creativity. As we have seen, the problem arises not so much from the existence of these debates—in fact this can be spiritually healthy—but from people's tendency to define spiritual fidelity by their own choice of cultural practices. In so doing they deny Christian liberty to their neighbor and launch new Christian culture wars.

LEAST UNDERSTOOD, LEAST PRACTICED

Despite the glaring need for it, Christian liberty may be the least understood and least practiced doctrine in the Bible. The reasons for misusing Christian liberty are as legion as the Christian pilgrims who walk the straight and narrow path. Not all of these reasons involve sin or spiritual immaturity, but some are rooted in self-righteousness. All of them in one form or another confuse *our practices* with *God's principles* to the detriment of *his purposes*. A few of the more obvious reasons why Christian liberty is not well understood or not practiced include the following:

1. *Christians confuse their absolutes with God's absolutes.* God has given us biblical principles for organizing our lives. These principles enunciate values and practices that define the Christian life, and we may reasonably expect other Christians' lives to be characterized by them. But, as we've seen, people add to God's list, absolutizing their own practices, then demanding that these practices be present in others' lives. Christian liberty is lost when Christians confuse their absolutes with God's absolutes.

2. *Christians honestly and legitimately differ on biblical interpretation.* In other words, Christians develop different and sometimes contradictory opinions, even moral perspectives, on varying issues. We dis-

cuss and debate issue interpretations but frequently deny each other
the opportunity to hold differing views without spiritual condemnation.

3. *Christians possess different personalities and come from different backgrounds, therefore developing different cultural practices.* Change and variety
are part of God's created order and no less so within the human race.
Christians like to do different things and tend to vest their own practices with greater significance or worth than the practices of others.

4. *Christians take seriously God's command to be not of the world.* In
their obedience, Christians sometimes zealously identify cultural
forms, methods, or practices they consider spiritually inappropriate.
In their desire to be not of the world, their list of condemned practices can get long.

5. *Habits and traditions create feelings of security.* This is a natural
human tendency. Habits are comfortable. Now it's easy to demonstrate that habit is not a sin in itself and thus is not an enemy of
the Christian faith. Some habits, called spiritual disciplines—like
reading your Bible and praying daily—are good things. But some
habits evolve into shallow ritualism, spawning "churchianity" rather
than biblical Christianity. Elsewhere I've called longtime habits traditions. Christian liberty is ignored when traditions become sanctified or are made sacred and are used as tests of true faith.

6. *Rules of behavior provide identity and, when codified, define the boundaries of the group.* This occurs when rules of behavior become rites
of passage. In Christian terms, we become more focused on the *rules*
of the church than on a *relationship* with Christ. The rules of behavior gradually take on a meaning as important as, or maybe superseding, the original principles they were designed to protect.

7. *Enforcing rules can be a form of spiritualized power.* The Christian
group in this instance assumes the form of a club. No one can be
part of the club unless he or she keeps the rules, and the rulers of
the club (church, denomination, religious subgroup) determine who
is in and who is out according to their interpretation of the rules.
This is much like the previous point. In the extreme, the *club* can
become a *cult,* threatening not only Christian liberty but also emotional or physical liberty.

8. *Our actions are frequently judged by others.* Elisabeth Elliot's experience with the Auca Indians led her to state the issue this way: "It
is not possible to behave in a way which would be understood by
all, let alone accepted by all. God alone, who is above all and in us

all, judges rightly, and therefore it is before him that we stand or
fall."[4] We will answer for our actions, right or wrong, not others'
opinions of our actions. Christian liberty is lost when Christians forget who is Judge.

  9. *Christians confuse convictions with preferences.* Christians entangle
biblically defined moral issues with cultural issues, which the Bible
does not address. Consequently, we sometimes fail to speak authoritatively about moral issues while we speak too authoritatively on
cultural issues.

  Christians become so confused on Christian liberty matters that
we create our own categories of "tolerable" and "intolerable" sin.
Theologically speaking, of course, there's no such thing as "tolerable" sin, which is by definition an offense to our holy and righteous
heavenly Father. But Christians create "tolerable" sins nonetheless.
"Intolerable" sins include murder, rape, or maybe grand larceny and
a few other really big sins. "Tolerable" sins include actions God calls
sin but we have learned to accept: unforgiveness, greed, bitterness,
gossip, unwholesome talk, pride, and even lying. We tolerate these
sins in the church even as we add to God's list of "intolerable" sins,
which might include voting for the "wrong" political party, fre-
quenting bowling alleys, using dice, and going to movie theaters or
any kind of theater.

CONVICTIONS AND PREFERENCES

  One of the ways we can sort the less important from the more
important issues is to learn the difference between *convictions* and
preferences. Convictions are those beliefs that are so central and so foundational to our life and practice that we are literally, should it ever
come to this extreme, willing to die in their defense. Convictions
have to do with essential, moral issues. They are the nonnegotiables
of our belief system. They are beliefs that we will not change and
should not change.

  For the Christian, convictions should be based on biblical principles, or what in the previous chapter I called God's holy list. At a
minimum, our convictions must include the moral absolutes of Scripture, such as worshiping only the one Lord, loving our neighbor as

ourselves, and remaining honest and sexually moral throughout our lives.

Preferences are those cultural practices that in our Christian liberty God *allows* us to embrace or espouse but that God does not *require* us to embrace or espouse. Preferences help create variety and richness in the body of Christ. Preferences are nonessential things and as such may differ from one Christian to another, one Christian group to another. They are the "'indifferent things,' things neither forbidden nor commanded by God."[5] Preferences are not on God's holy list, but they are on my list of desired standards and practices.

Our preferences typically include nonmoral issues or morally neutral matters. In conversational terms this simply means that such issues involve choices and practices that are not specifically forbidden in the Word of God. But we must be careful about designating anything that human beings believe or do as nonmoral, as if there are cultural activities in which human beings participate that are somehow not "religious" and consequently of no interest to the sovereign God. We've already seen that culture is religiously determined, for "there is no pure culture in the sense of being neutral religiously, or without positive or negative value ethically."[6] So even our nonmoral decisions, though small or less important than our moral decisions, emerge from our heart and must be evaluated for consistency with our Christian worldview. Nowhere am I implying that preference encompasses a set of issues or decisions that are beyond our accountability to God.

For example, some Christians have debated about unlucky days or numbers, considering this a nonmoral matter of preference rather than conviction. I would suggest, though, that this debate is not a matter of preference and is actually a violation of our Christian worldview. The belief in luck (and all superstition) is idolatry, a concept that is mutually exclusive with belief in the sovereign God. Christians who dabble with "luck," considering it a matter of liberty, evidence a deficiency in their theological understanding. There are no "lucky" Christians.[7]

We must be careful, then, to note that holding preferences is not wrong if and only if one's preferences do not themselves violate the revealed moral will of God. In other words, God gives us Christian liberty to develop our list beyond God's list, but our list must never contradict or otherwise undermine God's list of moral principles for our lives. Having standards or preferences does not make us legalistic. As long as our standards or preferences cohere with God's Word, then we can be considered people with character. Forcing our preferences on others as measurements of spirituality, however, means we're guilty of slipping into legalism.

Preferences may include such things as our likes and dislikes about fads (passing passions), food, or fashions.[8] In years gone by, Christians debated such preferences as courting without a chaperone, use—particularly by women—of bicycles, going to pool halls, use of motorcars, hairstyles— including male facial hair (still a perennial favorite)—mixed bathing, or Sunday observances, including but not limited to sports on Sunday, Sunday store openings and shopping, and Sunday newspapers.

More recently, preference debates have run the gamut of cultural expression. For Christians involved in these debates, though, the experience can feel more like running a gauntlet. Christians have disagreed rather vigorously about styles of music, use of syncopation in music, social or liturgical dancing, buttons or zippers on clothing, use of cosmetics, flirting and other public displays of affection, recreational gambling, opera, use of motorcycles, card playing, use of household appliances, smoking, use of sound equipment in church, singing without the use of hymnbooks, magic tricks (hand-is-quicker-than-the-eye illusions), kosher foods for Christians, drinking, grape juice or wine in communion cups, use of guitars or drums in the church, use of any instruments in the church, eating in restaurants that serve liquor, entertainment choices, hunting for sport, and women working outside the home.

Add to these the debates over Easter eggs, Halloween, and Harry Potter stories (are these about kids, candy, and harmless fantasy, or are they more about the occult and spiritism?), men's jewelry, participation in the dramatic arts, body piercing, and tattoos. There are more. Just look around.

THE CHRISTIAN LIBERTY OF ROMANS 14

God did not leave us without instructions on how to discern appropriate convictions and preferences or how to respond to different people's seemingly contradictory moral convictions. Romans 14 is the great Christian liberty chapter of the Bible (see also 1 Corinthians 8 and 10:14–33). More explicitly than any other passage of Scripture, Romans 14 describes how God wants Christians in all times, countries, and cultures to relate to one another's liberty in Christian love.

The Lord, through the apostle Paul (who refers to Christian liberty more than twice as often as other biblical writers, as in Rom. 6:17–18 and 2 Cor. 3:17), begins with a point-blank command: "Accept him whose faith is weak, without passing judgment on disputable matters" (Rom. 14:1).[9] Again in verse 13, Paul writes, "Therefore, let us stop passing judgment on one another." Passing judgment on disputable matters seems to be our key problem when it comes to Christian liberty. Christians just can't seem to resist "baptizing" our views and then judging others on that basis. In Romans 15:7 Paul reinforces his warning against passing judgment: "Accept one another, then, just as Christ accepted you."

Romans 14 details several more reasons why and how Christian liberty should be observed:

1. *Christians have differing levels of spiritual maturity.* That's what the apostle Paul means when he notes that one person's faith is weak (vv. 1–3). For the sake of Christian love and community, we must leave room for people to be different and to grow.

2. *Christians do not answer to each other; they are accountable to God.* "Who are you to judge someone else's servant? To his own master he stands or falls. And he will stand, for the Lord is able to make him stand" (v. 4). Later in the chapter: "For we will all stand before God's judgment seat. . . . So then, each of us will give an account of himself to God" (vv. 10, 12). This is individual accountability, as much a foundation stone of a free society as it is a key support of Christian liberty. This principle is balanced elsewhere in Scripture by our responsibilities in the community of the church, the "family of believers" (Gal. 6:1–10).

3. *Christians differ in their assessment of the spiritual significance of cultural events.* "One man considers one day more sacred than another; another man considers every day alike" (Rom. 14:5). James D. G. Dunn observed, "Two believers can disagree and yet both be right (that is, accepted by God). Given that we disagree, it is not necessary that you be wrong in order that I should be right."[10] Clearly, God leaves room for preferences. By the same token, having firm beliefs does not ipso facto make a person intolerant. If these beliefs do not

contradict Scripture, then, as we've observed before, you have a person of character who knows what he or she believes. Isn't the God of the Bible big enough to accept opposite convictions as well as preferences?[11]

4. *God expects Christians to use the reasoning capacity he has given them and make good choices.* "Each one should be fully convinced in his own mind" (v. 5b). And "Whatever you believe about these things keep between yourself and God" (v. 22). Christian liberty is exercised in community, but it is an individual privilege and responsibility.

5. *Christians are to make their choices "to the Lord."* This phrase is used six times in Romans 14:6–8. Freedom, like wisdom, begins with a fear of and submission to the Lord. If you regard a day as special, you do so "to the Lord." You eat or abstain from eating "to the Lord." We live "to the Lord"; we die "to the Lord"; we belong "to the Lord."

6. *The doctrine of Christian liberty provides not only for those exercising biblically defined freedom but also for those not yet ready to do so.* "Instead, make up your mind not to put any stumbling block or obstacle in your brother's way" (v. 13). In other words, Christian liberty never allows the strong to overrun the weak, never permits license in the name of liberty, never condones selfishness or self-righteousness, and never fails to acknowledge that even and especially in liberty Christ must be glorified.

7. *Nothing in God's creation is sinful in itself, but if one regards something as sinful, then to that person it is sinful.* "As one who is in the Lord Jesus, I am fully convinced that no food is unclean in itself. But if anyone regards something as unclean, then for him it is unclean" (v. 14). On each day of creation, God finished his work and saw that it was good (Genesis 1). "The earth is the LORD's and everything in it" (Ps. 24:1; 1 Cor. 10:26). If we know to do good and do not do it, it is sin, because "everything that does not come from faith is sin" (Rom. 14:20–23). These Scriptures make it clear that God created a perfect world, and he blessed it as very good. Too often, in an attempt to be more spiritual, Christians declare something sinful and off-limits that God never intended to be so. God gave us his creation to enjoy and he wants us to develop our culture within his creation to his glory.

8. *Christian liberty is guided by love.* Love does not limit liberty. Love works together with liberty to encourage fellowship (1 Cor. 8:9–13). No Christian who truly loves his neighbor as Christ has loved him will knowingly celebrate his freedoms in a manner that

causes the other to fall into sin. Such selfish behavior is incompatible with Christian love. Consequently, Christian liberty must sometimes be restrained for a season for the good of another. Unfortunately, most Christians would rather limit someone else's liberty than their own.

9. *The existence of criticism is not in itself a reason for limiting Christian liberty.* "Do not allow what you consider good to be spoken of as evil" (Rom. 14:16). The phrases "that causes someone else to stumble" and "cause your brother to fall" in verses 20–21 warn against behaviors that lead others into sin. The reason for limiting liberty is to protect a brother from *falling,* that is to say, falling into *sin,* not to bow to a brother's every pharisaical whim or criticism. In other words, the fact that someone does not like what you do is not in itself a reason to cease doing it. Were this the case, no one would do anything. "For why should my freedom be judged by another's conscience?" (1 Cor. 10:29). The key again is whether an action causes another to fall into sin. God wants weaker brothers to get stronger, not remain weak because stronger brothers bow to the weaker person's every whim. John Calvin said, "It is no less advantageous to our neighbors sometimes to use our Liberty to their benefit and edification than at other times to moderate it for their accommodation."[12]

10. *God's kingdom is about more than Christian liberties.* "For the kingdom of God is not a matter of eating and drinking, but of righteousness, peace and joy in the Holy Spirit, because anyone who serves Christ in this way is pleasing to God and approved by men" (Rom. 14:17–18). Whether we exercise Christian liberty or we do not, we are no better in the eyes of God (1 Cor. 8:8). What matters is our relationship with Christ.

11. *Christian community is important to God, and how we express our Christian liberty can directly affect the fellowship.* "Let us therefore make every effort to do what leads to peace and to mutual edification" (Rom. 14:19). The expression of your Christian liberty should edify or build up the Christian community, never tear it down. "Nobody should seek his own good, but the good of others" (1 Cor. 10:24). The exercise of our Christian liberty should never get in the way of the gospel.

So God has given us principles, which are timeless, rather than rules, which quickly become time-bound. Our task is to apply these biblical, God-given principles to all "questions of conscience" (1 Cor. 10:23–26).

Here we must take care. The old saw "Let your conscience be your guide" is poor advice. Our conscience is fallen (Titus 1:15). It is subject to the domination of Adam's sinful nature just like the rest of our being. It is given to human pride in a way that affects all of culture (see Gen. 11:4). So the guidance or advice we may receive from our own conscience is not always trustworthy (Rom. 8:5–8). That's why God said to be transformed by the renewing of our minds (12:2). Our conscience must be spiritually developed and Spirit-controlled (8:9; Col. 3:9–10).

MAKING CHOICES

In 1 Corinthians 6:12 the apostle Paul writes, "Everything is permissible for me—but not everything is beneficial. Everything is permissible for me—but I will not be mastered by anything." And again in 1 Corinthians 10:23, "Everything is permissible—but not everything is beneficial. Everything is permissible—but not everything is constructive." Clearly Paul is avowing once again the Christian doctrine that God created the world and everything in it, and it is good (Acts 10:15; Rom. 14:14; 1 Cor. 10:26). Humankind's dominion over culture is also good (Gen. 1:28–31). Paul is also acknowledging that Christ has set us free, but Christians must not use their freedom to indulge their sinful nature (Gal. 5:1, 13), and we are called on to make spiritually discerning decisions so that we can do what is best and be pure and blameless until the day of Christ (Phil. 1:9–11).

So we must ask ourselves, *Of all the things I could do, how do I decide what I should do?* Not everything is beneficial or constructive. Not everything builds us up. And Christians must never allow themselves to be mastered or controlled by anything—even if the activity is intrinsically innocent. Being "mastered" is subjection to idolatry. Some Christians, for example, should never seek access to the Internet, because they've discovered that they are unable to resist wasting hours in cyber surfing, or they are unable to turn away from available pornography. Perhaps there are others who are allowing their lives to be dominated by something recreational like golf. If they cannot participate at a level appropriate for them, they need, at least for a time, to stop playing golf. And so it is with any activity that dominates our attention and our time.

Christian liberty is not about doing whatever we want to do whenever we want to do it. It's neither a Christian version of hedonism nor a Christian form of situation ethics. Carl G. Kromminga asserts that Christian liberty or "moral discernment should seek out and command the things that really make a difference, the things (actions) that are truly advantageous, and this activity must issue from life."[13] Christian liberty choices are more about *free for* than *free from*.[14] Our Christian responsibility is to show the non-Christian world what freedom in Christ is really like, and our Christian opportunity is to influence culture with this same freedom that comes from our Savior who is Truth, Liberty, and Life.

One other ongoing obstacle to Christian demonstrations of liberty in Christ is the assumption that we must condone, approve of, or even like whatever other people do in the exercise of Christian liberty. For example, if a person who does not like drums in the church allows this liberty to others, the person assumes he or she must now enjoy drum playing in church. But this is not the case.

It's like granting each other freedom to eat what we choose. One person eats fettuccini. Another would never touch fettuccini but loves hamburgers. When was the last time you heard anyone's spirituality being questioned on the basis of what food he or she chooses to eat? It's true that in certain traditions only kosher foods are eaten or other food laws are observed, but for the most part this kind of spiritual judgment concerning food does not take place. Not only do we grant each other the liberty to eat whatever we like without judgment, we don't feel compelled to adopt another person's food choices as our own. Why don't we do the same with other matters of preference?

Nowhere in Scripture does it say that another person's Christian liberty choices must be your own. Nowhere does it say that we must like, adopt, endorse, or promote another person's preferences. What it does say, as we've already noted, is that we must stop passing judgment and allow room for others to exercise their Christian liberty before God, fully persuaded in their own minds. Whatever our neighbor's Christian liberty choices or preferences may be, we don't have to like them. Rather, we need to love our neighbor and let God be God.

The Strong and the Weak

Romans 14:20–21 reminds us that not everyone in the Christian community is at the same level of spiritual maturity in Christ. We are all in the process of becoming. Some are weak in the faith in that they do not possess the same depth of biblical knowledge or Christian experience or the same submission to the ministry of the Spirit in their lives as do stronger Christians (1 Corinthians 8). The weak are not without convictions, but they lack the ability to apply faith to their choices or they do not believe they can make certain choices.[15]

Strong Christians are enjoined by God to avoid using their Christian liberty in a manner that puts spiritual stumbling blocks in the way of weak Christians (Rom. 14:13–21; 1 Cor. 8:1–13; 10:23–33). A stumbling block or offense occurs only when some activity has the potential to induce a weaker brother to do something that his conscience does not permit.[16]

John Calvin distinguished between an offense *given* and an offense *taken*. An offense given is one that our actions cause, affecting only the weak. An offense taken is one that others construe to be offensive, even though the action was not malevolent or otherwise intended as an affront. In this case, people who take offense evidence what Calvin called "moroseness of temper and pharisaical superciliousness." Calvin further interpreted his observations for us, saying, "Wherefore we shall denominate the former, the offense of the weak, the latter, that of Pharisees; and we shall so temper the use of our liberty, that it ought to submit to the ignorance of the weak brethren, but not at all to the austerity of Pharisees."[17]

How much attention, then, should we give to the "Pharisees" and their "self-made purity"?[18] None. Let them alone, for they are the blind leading the blind and both will fall into the pit (Matt. 15:14).

The strong are not commanded to change their convictions but to hold them before God. Indeed, both strong and weak are admonished to "live to the Lord, so that differences in position do not result in differences in direction." Both the strong and the weak are to be tolerated if not embraced by the church. "For the strong to impose their convictions upon the weak would lead the latter astray, perhaps even to their eternal spiritual, moral destruction. And to impose the view of the weak on the strong would be to destroy the latter's Christian liberty."[19]

Consequently, Christian liberty may be used differently at different times out of a motive of love. A given choice, for example, may be required in public—before other believers—while not limited or proscribed in private.[20] We must always "study charity and keep in view the edification of our neighbors" (1 Cor. 10:24).[21] Those who are strong are expected to bear the failings of the weak and not please themselves (Rom. 15:1–2). We must avoid putting a stumbling block in the way of the weak brother. Yet John Calvin warned us to avoid yielding to pharisaical pressures: "It becomes us, indeed, to have regard for charity; but we must not offend God for the love of our neighbor."[22] There is a limit to how much we limit our liberty.

"[The] strong and weak need each other. Mutual service is patterned after Christ's service that has made believers members of his body, and this is effected by walking in the Spirit."[23] In his treatise of 1520, "On the Freedom of a Christian Man," Martin Luther wrote, "A Christian man is a most free lord of all, subject to none. A Christian man is a most dutiful servant of all, subject to all."[24] This is taught in 1 Corinthians 9:19–23. Paul said, "I have become all things to all men so that by all possible means I might save some. I do all this for the sake of the gospel."

Christian liberty is a marvelous gift of God. It's one way in which he reinforces the truth that human beings are made in his image. We are able to choose, and God commands us to make choices that are a spiritual act of worship.

LIFESTYLE LIBERTIES AND LIMITATIONS

The greatest test of a Christian's maturity is how he or she handles freedom. Christian liberty is about freedom in Christ, yet many Christians act as though their conscience is more constipated than emancipated. They are prudish or even puritanical, all in the name of Christian piety. They are the bickering spiritual siblings of Bible-believing churches-turned-spiritual-nurseries. They form legalistic, fossilized Christian subcultures or clubs with their own jargon, clicks, and clichés where new Christians and certainly nonbelievers cannot break in and may not even be welcome.

Others go in the other direction. They take freedom to its moral boundaries and beyond into license. This is no better than legalism.

Christians are born again to be free not to be wild (Gal. 5:13). License is a twisted liberty that takes us back to being "slaves to depravity" (2 Peter 2:19). License is pseudo-freedoms and counterfeits, like whim, greed, ego, and faddish passions. Folks who indulge in these forget that God said to avoid every kind of evil (1 Thess. 5:22).

John Calvin described these two perversions of Christian liberty: "For some, under the pretext of this liberty, cast off all obedience to God, and precipitate themselves into the most unbridled licentiousness; and some despise it, supposing it to be subversive of all moderation, order, and moral distinctions."[25]

Francis A. Schaeffer summarized the problem well when he wrote:

> It is my thesis that we cannot bind men morally except with that which the Scripture clearly commands (beyond that we can only give advice), similarly, *anything the New Testament does not command in regard to church form is a freedom to be exercised under the leadership of the Holy Spirit for that particular time and place.* In other words, the New Testament sets boundary conditions, but within these boundary conditions there is much freedom to meet the changes that arise both in different places and different times. . . . It is parallel to the evangelical church being bound by middle-class mores and making them equal with God's absolutes. To do this is sin. Not being able, as times change, to change under the Holy Spirit is ugly. It is the same in regard to church polity and practice: In a rapidly changing age like ours, an age of total upheaval like ours, to make non-absolutes absolutes guarantees both isolation and the death of the institutional, organized church.[26]

In a rapidly changing world, the church simply can no longer afford to wallow in debates over preferential issues, ignoring Christian liberty and abdicating its responsibility to think God's thoughts after him. We've been *freed from* the bondage of sin eternally, potentially *freed from* sin's grip day by day, and *freed to* apply the Christian liberty of our Christian worldview in a world enslaved by myriad false worldviews competing for followers.

God said to develop culture and to teach all nations. He said "Go," not "Stop" or "Hide" or "Hunker down." A world of opportunity awaits us.

6

MODERNITY
TO POSTMODERNITY

My times are in your hands.

Psalm 31:15

Star Trek, featuring Captain James T. Kirk and Mr. Spock, became a lasting cultural tour de force because it so engagingly portrayed the essence of Modernity—the values and aspirations of contemporary modern culture. Human reason and logic, scientific knowledge, and technology won the day for the crew of the USS *Enterprise* in each adventure they faced. Religion, if referenced at all, was relegated to less sophisticated humans or aliens on various planets but was never a part of the Federation starship's culture. Hope in the inevitability of progress was listed in the program's memorable opening lines: "These are the voyages of the starship *Enterprise.* Its five-year mission: to seek out new life and new civilizations . . . to boldly go where no man has gone before!"

Then culture changed. And so did *Star Trek.* The essence of Postmodernity was captured in subsequent cinematic and television spin-offs of the ever-popular series, including *Star Trek: The Next Generation,* beginning in 1987. *Next Generation* has Counselor Deanna Troi on the ship's crew. Regularly she gives advice to Captain Jean-Luc Picard based on her empathic abilities—her feelings of what another being might be doing or what a situation might demand. Also on the ship is the science officer, Data, an android who is better than human yet who wants to experience human emotions. In postmodern fashion, science and knowledge are not fully trusted. Captain Picard is as likely to take advice from Counselor Troi's feelings as he is from Data's technical knowledge.

In *Star Trek: Deep Space Nine,* beginning in 1993, Major Kyra Nerys, a key member of the crew, daily meditates (worships) before a candle shrine in her room and is quite open about her religious convictions. Several episodes revolve around her religion, prophets, and spiritual quandaries. Beginning in 1995, *Star Trek: Voyager,* featuring Captain Kathryn Janeway and Lieutenant Commander Chakotay, offered a program in which Chakotay, a man of Native American descent who carried a medicine bundle, guided the captain in a quest to identify her "animal-spirit guide."

In the later *Star Trek* series, as in postmodern culture, emotion, intuition, and spirituality, however vaguely defined, are once again considered acceptable parts of the cultural landscape. Science, technology, and progress are still evident in these later programs but are generally tinged with uncertainty. In the series we see a modern mentality give way to a postmodern mentality and we catch a glimpse of our own mixed hopes about a rapidly changing world.[1]

A RAPIDLY CHANGING WORLD

To become God's contemporary "men and women of Issachar," Christians need to understand both their Christian faith and their times, then apply Christian faith in the form of a Christian worldview to the questions and issues of their times. We've learned some things about a Christian worldview through the biblical teachings on change and order, on the necessity of spiritual discernment, and on Christian liberty. Now we need to look more closely at our changing times.

Our Christian worldview tells us God intervenes in history. We know that God is involved in both the biggest events of history, including the general course of grand social changes, and the most trivial events, like the flight of a small bird.[2] God exists, he has spoken, and he is active in the world. This truth should bolster our confidence so that we can interact with our times and the varied cultures within these times. When changing times make us feel like we can't see the forest for the trees, our knowledge of God should comfort us. In this age, we need all the spiritual confidence and comfort we can get, for both the forest and the trees are changing.

At an early age we all learn that change is, ironically, a constant of human life, affecting everyone. Intuitively we know that social change is inevitable. Empirically we can demonstrate it. The times change, and cultures rarely if ever stay the same from one period to the next. Very simply, *change is a social given, inevitable, inescapable, often irrevocable.*

The human life cycle is probably the most familiar and personal illustration of the maxim "Change is constant." You and I begin an aging process at birth, experience a soon-forgotten infancy, weather adolescence, and then march all too quickly through adulthood to old age and death. In the case of our human bodies, change is a biological imperative, an intrinsic dynamic in the nature of things physical.

Cultures change too. This happens because human interests and behaviors change. Take fads, for example. Fads fade away. They disappear. Are you still wearing bell-bottoms, spats, leisure suits, or Nehru jackets? Unless you're a real enthusiast, you're probably not still playing disco music. Have you or your friends bought a pet rock or a moon ring recently? Probably not. Do you even know what a pet rock or a moon ring is?

Issues come and go. Issues that once aroused passions steadily but surely become nonissues; then new questions, practices, and even whole lifestyles emerge. Remember the "Red scare" of the '50s? Remember beatniks, the war in Vietnam, and Women's Lib? Remember political debates about Jimmy Carter's malaise or Bill Clinton's "It's the economy, stupid"? Remember the infamous "hanging chads"? What does it mean to our culture that abortion-on-demand has been legal since 1973? When did we begin worrying about AIDS, computer viruses, or terrorists? Why doesn't anyone talk about thermonuclear war anymore? Clearly both our interests and the issues change. Human life is a forever-changing kaleidoscope of experiences—a series of new challenges and opportunities, new threats and frustrations, new joys and satisfactions.

Times change. Ancient Egypt is no more. Knights in armor no longer walk the earth. The cotton-ginned, slave-driven antebellum South is "gone with the wind." The Civil Rights Movement dismantled most of the Jim Crow laws in America. WASP America is rapidly browning, welcoming racially and ethnically diverse people from all over the globe. Back in the Victorian era, attitudes toward sexual expression and other forms of public decorum were substantially different from today's attitudes. Even language changes—hence the huge shift in Christian churches from the King James Version of the Bible to the New International Version or some similar, more contemporary translation.

Change seems to be as intrinsic to things social as it is to the physical or any other part of earthly existence. Change is ubiquitous.

PATTERNS OF CHANGE

To understand more than the "trees"—to really understand the "forest"—we need to learn to identify patterns of change in human history. A pattern, of course, is something that occurs in some related arrangement. Patterns of change are changes that occur in a related way within a period of time, and we can identify patterns of change by focusing on either *social continuity* or *social change.* Social continuity is sometimes called order and refers to social conditions or characteristics that persist throughout human history.

The Creator God is responsible for many examples of social continuity. Gender and human nature, for example, are forms of social continuity (Gen. 1:27). So is the family structure (2:24), religious activity and expression (4:3–4), the need for work (2:15; 3:19), the need for government (9:5–6; Rom. 13:1–7; 1 Tim. 2:1–2), or the basic human needs—food, shelter and security, sleep, sex and procreation, and significance. No matter what else changes, these fundamental characteristics of human life are always present from one century to the next.

But we want to learn more about social change, and focusing only on social continuity leaves us with an incomplete picture of the world and human history. It will help us to know that social change also occurs in varying scope, speed, and direction in every period of history. We may consider these changes as either positive or negative phenomena, depending on our presuppositions or our value judgments. For example, whether a person was an American colonist or a citizen of England in 1781 greatly influenced his or her view of

General Cornwallis's defeat at Yorktown. When Alexander Graham Bell invented the telephone in 1876, some hailed it as a breakthrough in communication, others as a useless toy that would soon be forgotten. Elvis, Buddy Holly, and later the Beatles launched a revolution in music in the 1950s and 1960s called rock 'n' roll that's been the focus of both animosity and affection ever since. Clearly change makes the world a complex, interesting, exciting, and yet sometimes difficult or unsettling place in which to live.

Technological innovation is another form of social change. Huge transformations in commerce, economics, language, and social customs have resulted from new technologies such as the printing press, the combustion engine, and computers.

Social change also may occur in less tangible but far more powerful ways. For example, the new ideas embodied in the Renaissance, the Enlightenment, and the Reformation affect us yet today. The liberation of the arts and sciences from medieval religious restrictions, a rediscovery of the doctrine of salvation by faith alone (the Reformation principle known as *sola fides* taken from Rom. 1:17), the inception of the Protestant denominational movement, and the Enlightenment elevation of trust in human reason are only a modest sample of the enormously influential social changes we've inherited from these periods of history.

We've learned that social change occurs at varying speeds and in a number of directions in every period of history. Our Christian view of social change informs us that it stems from new ideas, both people's moral and immoral choices, acts of God or other supernatural beings, and other social change. Since the ancient Greeks first thought about change, the recognition of change and the interpretation of it have been an enduring focus of all subsequent Western thought. We're always trying to find new ways to understand change, because something about change is fascinating.

When change occurs in patterns, it enables us to speak of "periods" of history. Several decades, even centuries, may be identified in which the changes that take place share certain common characteristics or are rooted in some specific philosophy regarding the world and humanity's purpose in it. Earl E. Cairns noted that the French philosopher Voltaire first coined the term *philosophy of history* and that it "is an attempt to interpret systematically the historical process by a principle that unifies the results of research and points to an ultimate meaning behind the process."[3]

To highlight some major characteristics deemed important in a given period of time, descriptive terms, such as *traditional, agricultural, Bronze Age, Iron Age,* or *Nuclear Age,* have frequently been used. The periods that we will focus on primarily here are the two most recent periods of social history, one called Modernity and the other called Postmodernity.

For an understanding of the period of history in which we live and the changes taking place around us, we need to examine a few somewhat challenging ideas and learn some new terms. I'll explain these ideas and define these terms as we proceed, but it's important not to get lost in the jargon. What matters is that we see what is changing and how it is changing. And then we must ask how our Christian worldview directs us to interact with the change.

Defining the Modern

First of all, let's think about the term *modern*. This word can be traced to early Latin usage in the sixth century when it referred to the contemporary. Webster notes that the word *modern* can be an adjective that means "of or characteristic of the present or recent times, not ancient," and it can be a noun: "a person living in modern times; a person having modern ideas, beliefs, standards, etc." In conversational terms we usually use the word *modern* to mean the here and now. In doing so, we are recognizing that some later time period is distinct from a previously known time period.

On the other hand, sometimes we use the word *modern* to refer to a certain set of new or contemporary ideas, beliefs, or standards identifiable in a person's thinking. Now we're acknowledging that not only has time passed, but also a new constellation of thoughts has emerged. Whether these new ideas are good, bad, or some hybrid of these extremes is a matter of value judgments stemming from our worldview. Simply stated, though, when we use the term *modern* this way, we're signaling that time is not the only thing that has changed.

Notice too that this use of the word *modern* is open-ended. We're making *modern* a synonym for the latest occurrence, for the new, and as such, it is a forever-moving, ever-fluid understanding of the "now." By making the idea of being modern a moving target, we're saying being modern can't be limited to just one fixed period of time.

This is confusing, for it suggests that *modern* could mean a certain outlook or way of behaving at a given period of time. Or *modern* could simply mean whatever is the latest and newest. So, for example, how long is art or architecture modern? Is it modern until some new artistic or architectural idea evolves, and then should we give it a new name because it's not modern anymore? Or is it modern forever, because at one time it was the latest development and the latest development is modern? This is part of the confusion with both the terms *Modernity* and *Postmodernity.* For several decades we've referred to our current historical period as Modernity, but now it's changing. So what do we call the new period? For want of a better term, we use Postmodernity—until someone suggests something better.

To the proverbial man on the street, being modern simply means being up-to-date, owning the latest gadget and knowing how to operate it. To younger folks, modern may mean being with it or doing the latest "in" thing. Older folks may think of modern as implying that "things just aren't what they used to be."

These popular conceptions of modern life share at least two attributes. The first is that they all speak of change. Somehow, to be modern, unlike during any other previous period of history, is to be conscious of change. And whether expected or unexpected, change in modern life seems to bring with it significant innovations in the way we view the world. It brings new knowledge, new human capacities to alter the environment, and new relationships. Each type of change seems to present a challenge all its own.

The second attribute that these conceptions of modern life share may be summed up in the word *gadget.* The modern person owns the latest gadget, and the latest gadgets may be what make some older members of society so aware of the differences in modern life. Of course, owning the latest gadget is simple enough because modern life has brought with it all manner of machines. In fact the very engine of modern life is technology.

I'll demonstrate my point by calling your attention to the word *engine* in the last sentence. So pervasive is mechanistic technology in modern life that no adult could read that sentence and fail to understand the metaphor. Technology, engines, and machines are integral to modern life.

We've identified two basic characteristics of the modern, or more specifically, what scholars have called Modernity. One is a consciousness of change, and the other is the presence of technology. But it is very important for us to understand that to many social philosophers, the term *Modernity* implies a great deal more than simply change or technology. In their writings, Modernity is a goal or an end to which all societies should aspire. Modernity is often represented, at least implicitly if not explicitly, as the final and best evolution of humanity, a kind of earthly utopia made possible by incredible advances in standards of living, knowledge, medicine, and technology. They believe that once Modernity is achieved, it will assuredly rid humanity of the limitations and frustrations of the human condition.

This view of Modernity is rooted in several philosophies, naturalism, humanism, and modernism among them. Together they have helped form the modern mentality. This modern mentality is rooted in certain philosophies but is both broader and more vaguely defined than these philosophies. It functions like a worldview even though it is generally not presented as a worldview. The modern mentality is something different from Modernity, a period of social history, yet its ascendancy makes it virtually synonymous with modern culture and Modernity.

Before we proceed, I want to be sure that we understand some things about our approach in this brief overview and some things about the concepts we're evaluating.

We know that we should apply our Christian worldview to social change.

We know that because of the effects of sin in this world, some change will be good and some will be bad.

We should remember that an all-or-nothing approach is not very helpful in Christian worldview thinking. We need to think more carefully than this.

We should keep in mind that Modernity and Postmodernity are very complex periods of social history, so we will not attack Modernity or Postmodernity, nor do we need to do so. Christians need not fear social change.

Christianity has influenced and is influencing these periods of history.

This said, it is very important for us to recognize that much of the philosophic and behavioral infrastructure of these periods of history is based on presuppositions, various "isms," and worldviews that are even antithetical to biblical Christianity. It can be confusing when non-Christians embrace a modern or postmodern mentality which is comprised of many non-Christian assumptions, then identify their views with Modernity or Postmodernity. Our Christian worldview may, therefore, call on us to reject aspects of Modernity or Postmodernity, not because we are rejecting an entire period of history or because we are against social change, but because non-Christian views dominate certain philosophies or activities within these periods of time.

Our task, then, is to understand something about Modernity and Postmodernity, to identify developments of either period and evaluate them in light of our Christian worldview, and then to enjoy culture before God even as we work to redeem for his glory the God-dishonoring aspects of culture. It is a challenging but not impossible task.

The Modern Mentality

The modern mentality is comprised of a variety of modern philosophies, borrowing from each yet not quite consistent with any one of them. Among modern mentality's primary influences are *naturalism, humanism,* and *modernism.*

Naturalism is the idea that the world can be understood in natural terms without recourse to the supernatural. *Humanism* is the Renaissance philosophy that emphasizes human capacity through reason, without the need for the supernatural or religion. *Modernism* is a philosophic affirmation of the future, something that is both different from and better than the past.[4]

These three philosophies create a *modern mentality,* the hallmark of which is "an existential conviction that man can select and can achieve his own future; that he has indeed many futures, that all he must do—to begin with—is to write his own scenario of the future as he himself dreams it and then to live his dream."[5] In other words, the modern mentality is not satisfied with the Christian doctrine that human beings are made in God's image; the modern mentality transforms human beings into God.

In addition, the modern mentality has adopted the Enlightenment perspective that "assumes that knowledge is not only certain (and hence rational) but also objective. The assumption of objectivity leads the modernist to claim access to dispassionate knowledge."[6] This means that individuals who embrace the modern mentality believe they can distinguish between truth and error and that they can do this without any biases that might stem from their own presuppositions or values. This understanding has paved the way for modern scientific worldviews.[7]

While the modern mentality increasingly has rejected God, it has maintained a belief in transcendence, purpose, design, ultimate reality, universal categories, and natural laws. The modern mentality also affirms the possibility of a unified field of knowledge (the idea that all knowledge somehow fits together in a coherent and consistent story) and assumes that meta-narratives (grand explanations for all reality) can be identified. It's as if the modern mentality borrowed God's attributes, transferring them to human beings or their culture, then discarded God as an "unnecessary hypothesis." These assumptions have allowed the modern mentality and the culture it helped create to develop a vast academic research industry, an incredibly productive capitalist economy, huge bureaucratic organizations, and a nearly unshakable faith in science and technology—and the probability of a better future.

You should understand that this modern mentality gives Modernity an enormous confidence, even arrogance, about the world and the future. The modern mentality encourages each man or woman to say, "I'll do it my way," and then he or she believes that whatever is tried will be accomplished.

The modern mentality really is more than a philosophy. It's both more and less than a self-consciously stated worldview; it's a state of mind that is diffused throughout popular culture and is identifiable in art, architecture, education, literature, music, politics, theology, science and research, and a number of other forms of human expression. This makes the modern mentality both a source and a product of Modernity.

Modernity

Modernity is a period of time, a culture, and, some say, a point of view. Some scholars believe that Modernity began in the early 1500s. Others reserve this term for the period beginning with the French

Revolution in 1789, following the Renaissance and the Enlightenment, and ending in 1989 with the fall of the Berlin Wall. Some equate Modernity with the Industrial Age, while others see it only as the twentieth century or even just the years post–World War II. Whatever beginning date you prefer, it's apparent that enough distinctive patterns of social change could be identified by the late 1800s to give this period the new name Modernity. Christianity played a key role in the development of Modernity. The rediscovery during the Reformation of Christianity's emphasis on the sovereign Creator and the Cultural Mandate liberated science and the arts to address the real world directly. Christianity's affirmation of work and a life's calling, respect for human dignity, protection of private property, and recognition of the rule of law strengthened capitalist economic systems and its attendant industrialization. Some of Modernity's central characteristics could not have developed without the truth of biblical Christianity working itself out in culture.

While Christianity's influence is apparent in modern life, and there is much about Modernity to commend it, the modern mentality and thus modern culture has increasingly drawn its primary inspiration from naturalism, humanism, and modernism. This shift is most evident in the modern mentality's clear embrace of "the proud Enlightenment belief that all of mankind's problems could be solved by autonomous human reason, freed from God's revelation."[8]

The modern mentality contributed to Modernity's frequent celebration of human achievement without reference to God. While God or, more vaguely, Providence was acknowledged in medieval and other traditional cultures, Modernity introduced a secular variant of Providence in the utopian belief in the inevitable progress of society.[9] The idea of progress became one of the dominant motifs of modern culture, along with its drive for power, production, and consumption via capitalist economies, affluence, fulfillment, and security.[10]

Modernity (being Mod, as it was called) and the process by which it develops—modernization—has been celebrated throughout the intellectual and artistic disciplines and has been called a time of "creative environment-mastering individualism."[11] Enthusiastic promoters of Modernity, ranging from educators to missionaries to politicians, have blurred the distinctions between the modern mentality and Modernity, thus making it increasingly difficult to evaluate one aside from the other. In their view a day had finally dawned in which humanity could rid the world of disease and difficulty, control the environment through science and technology, and achieve paradise on earth.

In time, the coupling of the modern mentality's presumption of human autonomy through reason with Modernity's seemingly unstoppable progress made it easier for individuals to embrace a steadily more virulent secular view of life. Secularism became both a social phenomenon and an ideology (almost a religion). In this way, secularization (the process of becoming more secular and less religious) emerged as an additional characteristic of Modernity.[12]

We'll understand secularization better if we know that three social developments are considered the primary causes for its development: *privatization*—the increasingly pronounced division of public and private life and the limiting of certain experiences like religion to private life; *pluralization*—the rapidly increasing number of moral choices available, including new faiths, ideologies, and worldviews; and *rationalization*—the increasing emphasis on human reason as the test of all truth drawn from science, and technology.[13]

Let's think about these developments again in the same order. First, in modern life, religion is steadily limited to the private sphere, thus diminishing its influence on the public sphere, social organizations, and culture. People learn to make social or public decisions without recourse to God, religion, church, or clergy. Religious convictions that once informed opinion on all issues in everyday life are now limited to "religious emergencies," such as weddings, tragedies, and funerals. In other words, many people, at least socially, choose to live as if God does not exist. A subconscious "practical atheism" or "informal agnosticism" becomes the rule of the day.

Second, the influence of religion in public life is being further diluted by a rapidly expanding list of alternative worldviews available in modern culture, each one claiming truth and clamoring for attention. And finally, dominating all of these worldviews is the modern mentality's affirmation of human reason as the ultimate source and test of truth, which in turn turns people away from religion and encourages secularization. All this combined creates a growing but generally ignored or denied crisis of belief in American culture and other modern societies.[14]

Scholars use the word *crisis* to describe a phenomenon heretofore unknown—a culture with seemingly no comprehensive or cohesive set of beliefs holding it together. It's a crisis in that people do not really know what to believe—yielding greater angst—at a time when they are being presented with more belief systems to choose from than ever.

The secularization of our society should not lead us to conclude that religion has gone away. Nothing could be further from the truth. Some Christian social observers like Peter Jones or J. A. Walter note that while forms of religious expression may have changed in the United States, religion is still alive and well. As J. A. Walter summarized it, people worship just as much as ever, but now there is a choice of altars.[15]

The modern mentality in both its secular and religious versions is identifiable in the cinema and in the arts, as well as in government.[16] In the academy, especially the modern public university, secularism in one form or another has long since replaced Christianity as the dominant educational philosophy.[17] New Age religion, neopaganism, spiritism and the occult, rediscovered Native American pantheism, reincarnation, renewed interest in the paranormal, and Buddhist or Hindu religious mysticism from the Far East are all forms of "religiosity," though not biblical Christianity.

Like all intellectual snapshots of social reality, Modernity helps us understand some parts of the social landscape while leaving some phenomena blurred and less recognizable. It may even leave some important parts of the social landscape completely out of the picture. This is important to remember, for history moves on. For some time now, some observers have been proclaiming the demise of Modernity and the rise of Postmodernity.

POSTMODERNITY

The term *Postmodernity* (often abbreviated to PoMo) was first used in the 1930s in reference to architecture. Since that time, Modernity has been roughly equated with the Industrial Age and Postmodernity roughly identified with the so-called Information Age. Many social observers, however, contend that the transition from Modernity to Postmodernity really did not get underway until the 1950s in the United States, Western Europe, and Japan. By the 1980s a fairly large body of observers agreed that Postmodernity had moved into mainstream culture.[18]

As we have seen, Modernity drew much of its strength and character from naturalism, humanism, and modernism, which helped create a modern mentality. Emerging Postmodernity is similarly forming around a new postmodern mentality, drawn largely from postmodernism. Postmodernity, the postmodern mentality, and postmodernism are not synonymous. But again, because postmodernism is so thoroughly related to both the postmodern mentality and Postmodernity—indeed, postmodernism fuels the postmodern mentality—it is difficult if not impossible to understand the one aside from the other.

Postmodernism refers to

> an array of cultural expressions that call into question the ideals, principles, and values that lay at the heart of the modern mind-set. *Postmodernity,* in turn, refers to an emerging epoch, the era in which we are living, the time when the postmodern outlook increasingly shapes our society. Postmodernity is the era in which postmodern ideas, attitudes, and values reign—when postmodernism molds culture.[19]

The *postmodern mentality* draws from postmodernism and may be expressed by individuals who have not recognized or formally embraced postmodernism but who nevertheless are influenced by a vaguely defined postmodern outlook.

Postmodernism recognizes no external moral authority.[20] In this view there is no God who is ultimate and sovereign. There is no universal explanation for why things are as they are in the world. There are no external or objective standards of right and wrong, beauty and ugliness, love and hate. Postmodernism suggests that the universe is simply "indeterminate" and that truth may not exist at all. Or if truth does exist, it is not absolute truth.

Stanley J. Grenz notes, "The postmodern mind refuses to limit truth to its rational dimension and thus dethrones the human intellect as the arbiter of truth." In addition, he observes that this postmodern mind "affirms that whatever we accept as truth and even the way we envision truth are dependent on the community in which we participate. Further, and far more radically, the postmodern worldview affirms that this relativity extends beyond our perceptions of truth to its essence; there is no absolute truth; rather, truth is relative to the community in which we participate."[21] In other words, postmodern "truth" exists only in a culturally conditioned way that makes it impossible to generalize across cultures, disciplines, or even from one individual to the next. "And since there are many human communities, there are necessarily many different truths. Most postmoderns make the leap of believing that this plurality of truths can exist alongside one another. *The postmodern consciousness, therefore, entails a radical kind of relativism and pluralism.*"[22] The relativism of the modern mentality was highly individualistic. It elevated personal taste and personal choice as be-all and end-all—"to each his own. . . . everyone has a right to his/her own opinion." In contrast, the postmodern mentality focuses on the group, a relativistic pluralism based on a local group's language, beliefs, and values.[23]

As a result, both postmodernism and the postmodern mentality foster a growth in global consciousness and the erosion of national consciousness. Nationalism suffers from increased loyalties to a more local geographic or demographic context, a kind of movement toward "retribalization." In the United States, for example, where American individualism has been a hallmark of the American psyche and culture, a new form of "group think" has emerged. Individualism still exists, but it tends to be focused through the lens of race, ethnicity, nationality, gender, so-called sexual orientation, and a variety of other forms of group consciousness. The motto now is "Think globally, act locally."[24]

Whether simply influenced by the postmodern mentality or thoroughly versed in postmodernism, people today do not know if knowledge is possible or, if it is, whether it is a good thing. Knowledge is not objective anymore; it is subjective, based on emotion and intuition. Reality is relative, indeterminate. The focus is on temporality and contingency, and logical and systematic thinking is rejected. Unlike the modern mentality, the postmodern mentality no longer believes that a meta-narrative of history is possible.[25] In other words, education, culture, and life itself must exist without a paradigm that gives meaning to the world in which we live.

In the emerging postmodern mentality, universals are out and particulars are in. Grand concepts like God or Providence may be useful from time to time but for the most part are not that important. Even progress, the prime directive of modern culture, is no longer trusted. In the postmodern mentality, nothing is really trusted.

Postmodernism and the postmodern mentality that it spawns assume that human beings are still autonomous, but progress is not inevitable after all. "Postmodernity emerges, we might say, at the point at which we face the fact that know-how and can-do may not always any longer so smoothly interlock as perhaps they once did."[26] This shift in attitude is so strong that we can almost (but not quite, because hope still exists) say that Modernity was about hope and Postmodernity is about despair. Clearly we can say that the post-modern mentality is keyed on uncertainty and the disillusionment that eventually stems from it. The Providence of premodern societies is said to have yielded to the progress of Modernity, and progress is now yielding to the pessimism of Postmodernity.

As early as 1888 Friedrich Nietzsche announced, "Nihilism stands at the door." This is a fatalistic denial that anything has ultimate or lasting meaning or purpose and is a rejection of all authority, laws, or tradition, which results in anarchy. He also announced his belief in the "death of God." By this he meant that we could no longer be sure of anything.[27] Since that time, varying forms of nihilism have become central themes in postmodern life.

The modern mentality celebrated *human autonomy* (God is not necessary), which is now yielding to the postmodern mentality's *human anomie* (there are no moral rules to live by), producing the *human angst* (acute anxiety about the world and personal freedom) that inevitably results. In the postmodern mentality, pessimism reigns over optimism.

The Modern/Postmodern

For a while now various pundits have been suggesting with mixed emotions that Modernity is collapsing. Certainly it is undeniable that Modernity is a culture in decline, but Modernity has not disappeared. Os Guinness says, "Modernism—as a set of ideas—may have collapsed, but Modernity—as a world system—is going strong."[28] Many of Modernity's central features—capitalism, industrialization, technology, telecommunications—are not likely to go away soon, and perhaps we do not want them to go.

It would appear that Postmodernity "refers to the exhaustion, but not necessarily the demise, of Modernity."[29] Consequently, we live in a culture in transition, one in which Mod and PoMo overlap, one in which a cacophony of voices vie for our attention. Perhaps we can summarize it best by simply listing what we think we know about the attributes, sensibilities, or patterns of this age:

Modernity

Assumed existence of objective truth; metaphysics

Faith in human reason, rationality, humanism, human autonomy, and individualism

Belief in transcendence, ultimate reality and universal categories, laws, meta-narratives, foundationalism, and the possibility of a unified field of knowledge

Themes of determinacy, purpose, design, being centered, objective

Faith in science and technology to control and develop nature

Idea of progress and its assumed inevitability; optimism, ultimate utopia

Themes of differentiation, hierarchy, rationalization, organization, bureaucracy

Secularization—religion and God unnecessary, distrusted, or at least privatized

Future orientation

Industrialization and technology of utmost importance

Urbanization

Postmodernity

Loss of confidence that truth exists; moral pluralism, and culturally determined "truth"

Nothing ultimately knowable; irrationalism, indeterminacy, chance

Human autonomy affirmed, but efficacy of human reason doubted; individual defined by the group; multiculturalism

Themes of immanence, subjectivity, experience, emotion, intuition, irony, psychotherapy, and the paranormal

Idea of progress doubted, even rejected

No meta-narrative of history possible; anti-foundationalism

Products of science and technology considered dubious at best

Desecularization via pagan spirituality, religiosity, vague spiritualism

Eclecticism, confusion, ambiguity, fragmentation, anarchy, and chaos embraced

Nonsequential and nonsystematic themes

Living in the now; loss of a sense of history

Deconstruction of language and political correctness

Themes of rootlessness and being decentered

Anomie, loss of direction or meaning, alienation; accepting a non-utopia

Diminished hope, pessimism, even despair; aloneness

Tribalism, terrorism, religio-culture wars prevalent

This brief overview of some of the key elements of Modernity and Postmodernity helps us understand just how thoroughly our times are changing. Social change in the early twenty-first century is extensive, and it involves some fundamental philosophic shifts that directly influence our lives. As we noted earlier, human beings always hunger for meaning and significance, no matter how much they may deny it, and culture is never devoid of religious content or ethical concerns. Of course the same is true for emerging postmodern culture. Our task now is to understand our times more thoroughly so that we will know how to live Christianly within them.

7

THE POSTMODERN CULTURE

Do not boast about tomorrow, for you do not know what a day may
bring forth.

Proverbs 27:1

From one man he made every nation of men, that they should inhabit
the whole earth; and he determined the times set for them and the
exact places where they should live. God did this so that men would
seek him and perhaps reach out for him and find him, though he is
not far from each one of us. For in him we live and move and have
our being.

Acts 17:26–28

The days of the Mod Squad are numbered. PoMo culture has
arrived in a pell-mell rush and with it comes a whole new
"worldview that denies all worldviews."[1] Given the demands
of everyday life, John Q. and Jane Public may not yet realize it, but
human understanding and expression are changing dramatically. No
civilized human endeavor remains untouched by the new cultus of
Postmodernity, whether religion, spirituality, philosophy, architecture, art and music, fads and fashions, literature, politics, or morality.[2]

Understanding the Times

Surely by now it should be evident to most of us that "to ignore the culture is to risk irrelevance; to accept the culture uncritically is to risk syncretism and unfaithfulness."[3] Christians need knowledge, and we need to act on this knowledge according to God's Word and will.

The Bible makes it clear that we must become proficient in "understanding the present time" (Rom. 13:11). God expects Christians to apply a distinctly Christian worldview in a manner that enables us to be in the world while not of the world, even as we go into the world for the cause of Christ.

PoMo culture is different from its predecessors in certain dramatic ways. Yet it is no different in that God is ultimately still in control, involved yet waiting until his purposes are fulfilled. As Christians, we must live out our faith in a way that glorifies God and challenges the moral inversions of PoMo culture. "Understanding the present time" reminds us that we are in a spiritual battle, perhaps one of the most morally confusing battles in human history.

But some of us are spiritually asleep. Gene Veith quotes George Barna's observation: "Most Christians ... do not perceive the Church to be in the midst of the most severe struggle it has faced in centuries." Veith goes on: "Many Christians, including theologians, are still battling modernism, unaware that the issues have changed. The Christians who minister effectively in this postmodern world and avoid its temptations will be the ones who understand the spirit of the age."[4]

Modernity's Swan Song?

At its zenith of popularity and power, Modernity was pictured by some enthusiasts of the modern mentality not simply as a period of history but as the final goal for all societies. Developed societies would be modern societies, and modern societies would be, by definition, developed societies. In this view Modernity represented a form of utopian human aspiration, a desire to ameliorate the human predicament by arriving at a point in history at which pain and problems are nonexistent. Modernity would produce heaven on earth.

As we've learned, the modern mentality that became so inter-twined with Modernity was founded on the belief that human rea-son alone was sufficient and ultimate. Reason, coupled with a Dar-winian understanding of the dynamics of nature, would produce unending technological, scientific, and moral progress, which in turn would make possible a sustainable quality of life appropriate for the self-actualization of all human beings.[5] Human beings were evolv-ing, always for the better.

Along the way, God would become nonfunctional, perhaps dys-functional, because the modern mentality's naturalistic presupposi-tions ultimately attempted to eliminate God from consideration. The very heart of the spirit of the modern mentality and by implication Modernity was a desire to be autonomous or free from God.

There was only one problem with all this. It didn't work. Nor could it ever work. By putting God outside its philosophic box and then eventually denying that God existed, the modern mentality suc-ceeded only in creating a new sovereign. Without God, it is inevitable that some part of the human experience will become absolutized and human beings become enslaved to deterministic, socially con-trived substitutes for God, whether society, history, time, econom-ics, or the environment.

These core ideas of the modern mentality helped produce a twen-tieth century version of Modernity, characterized by both helpful and harmful developments: continuous social change, technological innovation—first the motor and the engine, then the computer—medical advancement, the Great Depression, world wars of mass destruction, the Holocaust, social unrest and the counterculture, legalized abortion, and rising domestic crime and violence, to name only a few. It was a century when *what could be* was divorced from considerations of *what ought to be*.

While God has allowed the creative spirit of humanity to discover and develop many good things in the modern period, Modernity will always be remembered as a period of evil writ large. Though Modernity is still around, overlapping the postmodern period, even-tually it will "return to dust"—undoubtedly during this twenty-first century. When this happens, the epitaph on its tombstone will likely be "A time of great good, a time of greater evil."

Needless to say, postmodernists—meaning those who embrace the postmodern mentality, whether they know it or not—are react-ing to the modern mentality's hyperconfidence in human potential and overstated faith in reason, science, and progress. A new PoMo culture is turning away from strict adherence to rationalism, scientism, technicism, and even secularism. And postmodern culture is characterized by a new postmodern mentality that searches for meaning not in a *rejection* of "moral notions" but in an *embrace* of multiple moralities.[6] "For postmoderns the question is not so much 'Is there a God?' but 'Which God?'"[7]

MORAL PLURALISM

Postmodern culture's defining characteristic is the heresy variously known as moral pluralism, moral relativism, or simply relativism. Under whatever name, this set of beliefs is becoming what Stanley J. Grenz called "the central hallmark of postmodern cultural expression."[8]

It would appear that moral pluralism resonates well with the democratic ideals on which this country was founded. Pluralism is something that we've always valued in America. It's part of and essential to the Great Experiment known as a free country "of the people, by the people, and for the people." Politically it means that people from different backgrounds or groups are given an equal opportunity to enjoy the fruits of freedom. It signifies and protects both religious and political liberty. Indeed, "religious liberty makes pluralism more likely; pluralism makes religious liberty more necessary."[9]

As our country was being born, political pluralism meant, at least in theory, that different groups, even factions, were valued because of the strength produced by many groups joining to form one nation. This is one of the fundamental characteristics of a republican form of government, something James Madison so eloquently addressed in *The Federalist Papers* and which is evident in the United States of America's national motto—*E Pluribus Unum*, "out of many, one."[10]

The glue that held this nation of many groups and individuals together was allegiance to a set of ideals or values. In other words, the nation became a nation not just because a great number of people occupied the same geographic space but because those people shared a common philosophy about what was right and wrong and about what was good for their children. So political pluralism is a powerful product and ally of religious liberty and a guarantor of political liberty. In itself, political pluralism need not entail moral pluralism or relativism. In fact political pluralism needs moral foundations and clarity to preserve individual and group freedom. But the emergence of postmodern culture in the late twentieth century has introduced a new definition of pluralism.

Americans are applying the idea of pluralism to morality, or more specifically, to morality as it influences ethics, education, medicine, and the law; and the results are disastrous. The sacred canopy is rapidly being lost and the emerging naked public square leaves postmodern culture without a sense of center or direction.[11] Where once we were varied groups, differing on political questions but held together by a public moral consensus on what constitutes ultimate values of right and wrong, now we're witnessing the fragmentation of society as individuals pull away from other individuals because few moral values are commonly embraced.[12] Along with, and at times supplanting, a *desirable political pluralism,* we now have a *dangerous moral pluralism.* It's this condition that leads to social fragmentation, which may easily degenerate further into disintegration.

Where once all agreed that everyone was entitled to his or her own opinion in the search for truth, now moral pluralism argues everyone is entitled to his or her own truth.[13] Short of an outright denial of the existence of God, there is no more significant a cultural paradigm shift than this. The result is not the disappearance of faith but rather the loss or devaluation of its cultural authority and the cultural disorientation that follows.[14]

Moral pluralism (or moral relativism) allows for belief in God and in gods but defrocks the Supreme Being of his supremacy and, ostensibly at least, knows no absolutes, no ultimate standard of fact or fiction, no limitation or restraint. "Relativism is the belief that truth and error, right and wrong, beautiful and ugly, normal and abnormal, and a host of other judgments are determined by the individual, her circumstances, or her culture."[15] In Postmodernity's version of moral pluralism, decisions about right and wrong are based on personal preference, situation ethics, or what have come to be called quality of life or lifestyle considerations. For some, postmodern ethics is purely a matter of self-invention (think about rock star Madonna or Bill Clinton).[16]

Moral pluralism's principal self-contradiction is its assertion that there are *absolutely no absolutes.* Because of this assertion, some have argued that moral pluralism is really not the correct term, that one set of absolutes based on a broadly defined Judeo-Christian heritage has simply been replaced by another set of absolutes based on the syncretism of naturalistic, humanistic, and pantheistic philosophies and pagan New Age spirituality.[17] This argument has merit, for it illustrates the great irony of postmodern moral pluralism. Its relativistic assumptions are applied absolutely. This is never clearer than in deconstructionist assertions regarding power and political correctness or discussions about tolerance in which tolerance is offered to virtually any belief system except biblical Christianity.

While moral pluralism is presented as a new freedom, it is little more than the beginning of anarchy—everyone doing what is right in his or her own eyes, leading to what Os Guinness calls a "perpetually fractious society."[18] Moral pluralism grants plausibility to anything, but "granting plausibility to anything also means granting certainty to nothing. The spirit of relativistic pluralism indicts certainty and firm convictions as 'close-minded.'"[19] So the postmodern mentality rejects biblical Christianity not so much because it claims to know truth (for everyone is entitled to his or her own truth) but because of Christianity's claim to exclusive and objective truth.

In postmodern culture, for the first time in history, a significant number of individuals believe people should play a role in defining their own morality. Alan Wolfe describes this state of mind:

> The defining characteristic of the moral philosophy of Americans can therefore be described as the principle of moral freedom. Moral freedom means that individuals should determine for themselves what it means to lead a good and virtuous life. . . . *The ultimate of the idea of moral freedom is not that people are created in the image of a higher authority. It is instead that any form of higher authority has to tailor its commandments to the needs of real people. . . . The idea of people having the freedom to choose their own way of believing . . . assumes that the individual is in charge of his own destiny. . . .* Far from a land populated by secular humanists, Americans want faith and freedom simultaneously.[20]

THE POSTMODERN MENTALITY

The postmodern mind-set "is unique among avant-garde movements in that it appeals not to an artistic elite but to all those engaged in activities of daily life through popular culture and the mass media."[21] "The pop culture of our day reflects the centerless pluralism of Postmodernity and gives expression to the antirationalism of postmodernism."[22] The postmodern mind-set is everywhere, even as it goes nowhere.

Indeed, the postmodern mentality is centerless. "No clear shared focus unites the diverse and divergent elements of postmodern society into a single whole. There are no longer any common standards to which people can appeal in their efforts to measure, judge, or value ideas, opinions, or lifestyle choices." The postmodern mind-set is more than morally pluralist. Particulars matter. Now culture does not just embrace the tolerance of differences, culture celebrates diversity. Eclecticism is the postmodern style.[23] With its host of sideshows and no center-ring attraction, the carnival has become the new metaphor for postmodern life.[24]

Stanley Grenz gives us an example:

> Above all, the postmodern outlook is evident in what is called "bricolage." In pointed defiance of the traditional attempt to coordinate individual pieces of clothing in a unified look, the postmodern style intentionally juxtaposes incompatible or heterogeneous elements, such as garments and accessories from each of the preceding four decades.[25]

As a consequence, current clothing styles mix elements that were considered incompatible before. This is not happening merely from a lack of care but is intended to produce an ironic effect or parody of modern fashion norms.

The same is true for belief systems. We create our own collage of beliefs. In postmodern culture, you can believe in classic church doctrines at the same time you embrace traditionally non-Christian ideas like reincarnation. Our neighbors consider beliefs just a matter of social context, so it causes them no intellectual dissonance if the tenets of their worldview are inconsistent.[26] Today you can believe whatever you want to believe.

In some quarters of our society, secularization continues to advance but is essentially a dying movement left over from Modernity. Today, rather than being required to worship God (premodern) or expected to disown God (modern), we are encouraged to choose our own God (postmodern). Postmodernity has multiplied the smorgasbord of worldviews considered viable so that generally people believe in some kind of god, embrace a few residual tenets of Christianity found lying around the cultural table, add whatever other religious views seem appealing to them, then go on with their lives in a religiously minimalist manner.

The distinction between fiction and fact has evaporated, and this affects our understanding of knowledge, of course. But it also affects the way we think, for there can be no logical structures if no choice is considered more rational, more coherent, better, or wiser than another. Everything is transitory, fleeting, subjective, even the meaning of words, mathematics, biochemistry, and life itself.

At a time when so many sets of values are available for the choosing, people don't seem to have confidence in any values at all. As I said earlier, this kind of religious relativism is resulting in a fragmenting, if not deteriorating, culture. Both at the popular and the intellectual level, secular worldviews have not been able to answer humanity's inner need to know why. So the emerging postmodern culture finds it difficult to share the self-righteous and smugly hopeful image of the modern era.

> Where modernism was a manifesto of human self-confidence and self-congratulations, postmodernism is a confession of modesty, if not despair! There is no truth, only truths. There are no principles, only preferences. There is no grand reason, only reasons. There is no privileged civilization (or culture, beliefs, norms, and styles), only a multiplicity of cultures, beliefs, periods, and styles.[27]

Postmodern Sensibilities

Even the term *Postmodernity* indicates something of the bewilderment that has overtaken formerly confident and self-assured people with a modernist mentality. No one seems to know what to call this age. It's just post—something other than what it has been. If the zeitgeist of the modern era was one of hope in human accomplishment, the zeitgeist of the postmodern period seems to be confusion, despair, or resignation.

Let's step back for a moment, though, and test our perspective. Postmodernity is a period of time in history. As such, it is no more (or less) threatening to Christian people and a Christian worldview than any other period of time. Thinking just of a period of time, Christians are postmoderns. It's unavoidable. If you're alive and you're in the world, you're a postmodern. But that doesn't necessarily mean that you espouse postmodernism or even that you are greatly influenced by the postmodern mentality.

It's very difficult for me not to use the terms *Postmodernity* and *postmodernism* interchangeably. But, as I pointed out in the last chapter, the two concepts, along with the postmodern mentality they spawn, are not the same. Using these words interchangeably perpetuates confusion. For example, Charles Colson decries postmodernism and a popular theologian who told a conference audience, "Don't fight Postmodernity." Colson writes, "Postmodernism must be confronted, not accommodated. We must challenge its false presuppositions, lovingly explaining that there is truth and that it is knowable."[28]

Meanwhile Brian D. McLaren says, "Opposing postmodernism is as futile as opposing the English language. It's here. It's reality. It's the future. It's not only a fact on the event horizon; it's the way my generation processes every other fact on the event horizon. What are we going to do about it, with it, in it?"[29]

I cannot speak for these men, but if I understand their writings, I'd suggest that they agree on much about a biblical, evangelical Christian faith. But they are using the term *postmodernism* differently. Postmodernity per se is not the issue. Postmodernism is. Postmodernism is a philosophy, and, fully stated, it's a worldview. The postmodern mentality is a cultural borrowing from postmodernism, influencing many people who otherwise may not embrace certain tenets of postmodernism.

We should remember that Postmodernity (like Modernity) is not monolithic and not all of its expressions are necessarily antithetical to a Christian philosophy of life. Neither modern nor postmodern culture is uniformly Christian or anti-Christian. Nor are all postmodern developments bad or uniformly objectionable. Rejection of some elements of postmodern culture does not imply that all should be rejected. Nor does criticism of postmodern culture imply an uncritical acceptance of modern culture. All culture must come under the critical review of biblical truth.

Some new developments in this postmodern period might be attractive—renewed interest in the supernatural, a rejection of some of the anti-Christian themes of modernism and Modernity, and a rediscovery of creativity in the human spirit, for example. In addition, God always has his remnant of believers who salt and light their culture with the optimistic realism of biblical Christian truth. Whether Postmodernity is post-Christian is subject to debate, but one thing is clear: To function at all, cultures always live on what Francis A. Schaeffer frequently called "borrowed Christian values." So while our description of postmodern culture may at points seem overly dark, it still recognizes that people are *imago Dei* and God is on his throne.

All this discussion of terms and meanings may seem like an academic or esoteric exercise, but a little understanding of their differences should go a long way in helping avoid confusion in the Christian community as we discuss culture and determine just what is the "enemy."

Now we must understand that insofar as Postmodernity is greatly influenced by or perhaps even characterized by a certain set of beliefs— like postmodernism or a vaguely but widely adopted postmodern mentality—Postmodernity must be carefully considered by thinking Christians who wish to fulfill their responsibilities before God.

That said, we must acknowledge that the dominant sensibilities of postmodern culture, drawn from postmodernism, form a world-view or at least a postmodern mentality largely contrary to biblical Christianity. This postmodern mentality is broadcast in media, presented in art and literature, marketed in business, performed in music, preached in politics and the pulpit, and taught in universities.

The postmodern mentality's moral relativism spawns both a new openness to discussion of religious faith and also new cultural conceits and degradations. It's this reality that may be causing some to reconsider the claims of historic orthodox Christian belief. But it is also this reality that drives many people further into rootlessness and pessimism, whether religiously or profanely expressed.

A few postmodern intellectuals still tout the glories of science and technology and the arrival of Postmodernity as their cosmological hope. No need for God here. On the other hand, many other intellectuals are quite confused and disillusioned, something intellectuals in the modern period are not accustomed to being—or at least admitting. Some have virtually lost all hope while others still place their hope in human resilience.

Postmodern culture's perspective is rooted in the faith either that God does not exist or that you may choose to believe in whatever god you wish. Once you accept the idea that God does not exist or that his existence or power is irrelevant, the only thing left is moral relativism. Once you accept moral relativism, only two paths remain open to you philosophically and practically. One is *hedonism,* and the other is *nihilism.*

Hedonism is the belief that life's highest good is pleasure, that life is about pleasure, and that you may give your life over to an unfettered pursuit of pleasure, however you may define it. This view of life knows no principles or parameters, so it's not an expression of pleasure in such things as a family Christmas, a wedding, the salvation of a loved one, or the birth of a child. Hedonism is a maximization of immoral recreations, including promiscuity, gluttony, drugs, and other aberrant behaviors. Hedonism is livable for a time, until the accounts receivable of your sin—physically, emotionally, spiritually, or otherwise—must, inevitably, be paid.

Nihilism is Nietzsche's fatalistic "certain uncertainty," the idea that we cannot be sure of anything. What's going to happen will happen, and there is no meaning beyond this. For the human heart, divinely designed as it is for eternal significance in relationship to God, nihilism is an unlivable condition. While people try, no human being can live for long with nihilistic assumptions. The rock group Smashing Pumpkins described these hopeless people as just "rats in a cage." Nihilism is embodied in shock rocker Marilyn Manson. Such people hammer themselves in abject despair, masochistically painting and piercing their bodies, escaping temporarily by bingeing on foreign substances, risking, even inviting, disease via sexual deviancy, or, finally and frequently, committing suicide, like Kurt Cobain from the grunge group Nirvana.

A strange admixture of hedonism and nihilism is presented daily on MTV, the now more than twenty-year-old audio/video bible of the youth of PoMo culture. Since the world is arrayed against them, youth are told to live their lives without authority, getting what they can get. Women are property, toys, objects of sexual fantasy and fulfillment, and "hos"—just commodities to be exploited and abandoned. Love equals sex and sex equals love—if love exists. Aggression, anarchy, violence, murder, sadism and masochism, illegal substance use and abuse, chauvinism, libertinism, sedition, power or powerlessness, and seduction ground the attitudes and actions that are given extensive airtime. Undergirding all these expressions is anger. Anger at what? Anger at existence, at authority, and at a deep-seated feeling that life itself has no meaning.

MTV's postmodern ethic may be vulgarly expressed, but it's merely the more extreme of the attitudes and values now found throughout PoMo culture at all levels of presumed sophistication. For example, if there is no God who is truth, we find our identity only in demography—our race, gender, nationality, or ethnicity. Individuality is lost in the definition of the group. The tribalistic thinking of countless subgroups of people—anyone who can find a differentiating but mutually identifying factor—regularly evidences itself not just in hobbies and other healthy outcomes of free association but also in demands for special rights. The melting pot becomes the salad bowl, which becomes the patchwork quilt or kaleidoscope of culture. In the more activist forms of multiculturalism, all cultural subgroups are considered morally equivalent. So in what is now being called cultural diversity, Christians must insist that each culture and each practice be critiqued on its own merits before the righteous and transcendent God of truth.[30]

The adolescent emotionalism and moral relativism of MTV can also be seen on television talk shows and "reality" programming. The relational chaos of MTV is a youth-oriented microcosm of the broader culture's hedonism and nihilism expressed in high divorce rates, deadbeat dads, alcoholism, affairs and adultery, gambling excess, or conspicuous consumption.

The bottom line is this: Social change that seemed so directed toward improvement of the human condition in the modern era is now producing much more questionable, if morally predictable, results. A hope that seemed so defensible, logical, and self-evident to Modernity—discernable even in the music of the sixties' counterculture—now seems vain, and this is painfully apparent in the music, art, drama, and literature of the current culture.

Centrifugal Forces

Postmodern moral relativism creates an upside-down culture. It's a centrifugal force that pulls the culture apart. We can see moral relativism in the nation's city streets where young men (and increasingly young women) in gangland surrogate families live and die by the code "Might makes right." If we follow moral relativism, we cannot tell teenagers that it's wrong and destructive to be sexually active outside of marriage, because that would mean having a standard, and moral relativism recognizes no standard but preference, individual choice, or so-called tolerance.

New forms of bias and discrimination, ironically in the name of tolerance and diversity, have developed on American university campuses with the advent of speech codes, lists of words or phrases that someone deems offensive or insensitive. In the name of tolerance, free speech gives way to controlled speech, a new form of intolerance. Deconstructionist revisionist scholars engage in demythologizing, decanonizing, and dehegemonizing any written literary texts because they no longer believe words have any objective meaning. In this view texts are just stories and do not and cannot contain knowledge, so the process of learning a deconstructionist worldview is all that matters and in many courses is all that's taught.

Perhaps it is time to take the gloves off. Anyone who thinks that education is value free is seriously misinformed. You can receive an education in a public or independent institution of higher learning, but unless you are enrolled at an avowedly Christian college or university, you will not receive a Christian education. If you're not receiving a Christian education, you're receiving some other kind of worldview education. Most often the worldview being instilled in this generation of college students is one based on postmodern thinking.[31]

Postmodernity's paradoxical worldview is difficult to fight because, as we've seen, it is by definition syncretistic. It's the collage of sometimes simultaneously held contradictory or inconsistent beliefs. Postmodernity recognizes no absolutes but those that are in vogue at the moment. For example, while virtually any worldview but the truth-claims of biblical Christianity is acceptable (especially in the academy), thoughtful postmodernists typically maintain their own list of sins. These might include, for example, being closed-minded, using politically designated hate speech, or praying in public settings. (Following the 9/11 tragedy, however, prayer temporarily moved out of the "sin" category.) Meanwhile a long list of sexually deviant behavior is considered acceptable, even laudable, and various forms of superstition, paganism, or pantheism are celebrated as open-minded and chic.

Postmodernism's moral relativism is defining the emerging postmodern mentality and dominating Postmodernity. It is, perhaps, more difficult to fight than any other kind of foe. As I wrote several years ago, "This enemy has no country, no political party, no army, no uniform. Moral relativism presents no immediately recognizable threat to our physical safety. But the idea of relativism is just as threatening as any past enemy has ever been. Indeed, moral relativism may be a greater enemy because it attacks the mind and the heart."[32]

INDIVIDUALS MATTER

If somehow we could continue to speak of social change in cultures or ages as only abstract, impersonal, and far-away events, then perhaps we could rest assured that our lives would not be disturbed by it. But this is not the case. Cultures are manifestations of individuals' activities, and ages are but a record of individuals' interests and efforts in time. Individuals matter.

Yet the social forces we've described as characteristic of Modernity and now Postmodernity take on a life of their own that seems to transcend the individual. Often human beings become a kind of social fallout. For individuals, if there are no absolutes, then there can be no sense of self, no fixed identity for human beings, because God created us with a God-consciousness and a need to know him to know ourselves. Consequently, the mood of postmodern culture moves beyond despair to panic, a free fall that comes with "the disappearance of external standards of public conduct . . . and the dissolution of the internal foundations of identity."[33] The result is cynicism.

PoMo culture doesn't seem to have a purpose, so a thoroughgoing pessimism or cynicism afflicts the contemporary mood. In plain and simple terms, people hurt. Spiritually and emotionally people are seeking solace but in a lot of wrong places.

So the sum of the matter is that postmodern men and women are trapped in a worldview cul-de-sac of their own making. Comprehensive social change casts aside human beings like flotsam and jetsam. In this context in which people feel like they don't matter, social change loses its abstraction and its impersonality, because men and women as individuals have a value that exceeds the abstraction called society and the culture in which they live. Terms like *Modernity* and *Postmodernity,* which sounded like so much jargon, now become powerful descriptions of human need.

But postmodern culture is complex, contradictory, and confused. There are cracks in its armor. With a Christian understanding of social change, we know the truth that even Postmodernity will not last long; it too will change. And we can trust in the sovereign God's loving willingness to redeem and reconcile those who thought they had destroyed the foundations (Ps. 11:3).

Meanwhile a lot of Christians aren't much help when it comes to dealing with the realities of Postmodernity, for they are in a cultural cul-de-sac of their own, fighting their own culture wars and missing the larger, more important battles of their times.

8

CHRISTIAN CULTURE WARS

For the kingdom of God is not a matter of eating and drinking, but
of righteousness, peace and joy in the Holy Spirit.

Romans 14:17

D ealing with social change has never been a Christian strong
suit—primarily, I believe, because too few Christians have
ever really developed a Christian worldview. Contemporary social researcher George Barna says, "An unbelievably small por-
tion of believers have what is called a Christian worldview . . . and
because (most Christians) don't think like Christians, they can't act
like Christians. Because they don't act like Christians, they can't have
much impact on the world in which they live."[1]

So Christians stop short of developing a biblically based Christian worldview and are consequently motivated by something other
than the "whole will of God" (Acts 20:27). When we do this we're
susceptible to all manner of influences on our thinking. We're in the
world, but we're not able to fulfill Christ's injunction to be not of
the world. If we are of the world, we are of our culture. We think
and act indiscriminately like those around us. Since sin and the fall
have perverted our cultural motivations, instead of serving God, we
now serve ourselves. For Christians, just like nonbelievers, this biblically uninformed action becomes a form of idolatry and rebellion
against God.[2]

Inevitably, the weaker our Christian worldview, the stronger our allegiance to the cultural forms of our time. When the current zeitgeist exercises more influence over our actions than the Spirit of God, our values, views, and actions become more cultural than Christian. Then the highly individualized opinions of Christians or the varying views of Christian factions and subgroups destroy the unity available via the Spirit of God who indwells every believer. The disunity of our culture subverts Christian unity.

Even though Christians know that "where the Spirit of the Lord is, there is freedom" (2 Cor. 3:17), we too frequently choose the false freedom of other worldviews, which in the end leads only to enslavement to cultural forms. Then we think and act like nonbelievers. Without submission to the Spirit, there is ultimately neither unity nor real liberty. Without a developed Christian worldview, there is no ability to critique culture and be not of the world. Disunity and the inevitable Christian culture wars are the result. Sadly, this is nothing new. The wisest man who ever lived once said, "There is nothing new under the sun" (Eccles. 1:9). This seems like an odd remark to include in a text on rapid social change. But King Solomon was right, especially as this observation applies to human nature and behavior.

Christians, being human, are part of the picture, and in the case we're examining here, part of the problem. In his magnum opus, *A History of Christianity,* the great historian Kenneth Scott Latourette easily demonstrated that Christians have conducted and participated in innumerable culture wars throughout the past two thousand years.[3]

Christians "lob and rob." They lob verbal grenades of judgment at other Christians with whom they differ, judging others' spirituality and thus ignoring Romans 14:13. By so doing, they rob themselves and others of Christian joy. And perhaps even more important, they rob themselves of an opportunity to share Christ as the way, the truth, and the life with a culture bereft of biblical and moral focus.

As it was in the past, so it is today. Without a developed Christian worldview, Christians continue to struggle with social change, lose their unity in the Spirit, and turn inside the church to fight internecine culture wars. Without a biblically structured Christian worldview and without the unity of the Spirit, Christians, like non-Christians of our society, balkanize into countless factions defined by their own customs, traditions, cultural forms, or idiosyncratic practices—virtually anything that creates a kind of community, but one that knows neither real truth nor real liberty.

This loss of true Christian community is tragic enough in itself, but it gets worse: The more Christians reflect the postmodern culture in which they live, the more they offer no authentic alternative to the nonbeliever. Postmodern nonbelievers—our neighbors whom God said we should love—see that Christian churches and other forms of Christian community are just as immersed in cultural chaos as the world. So what would attract or convict the nonbeliever's heart? Very little. Meanwhile, Christians go blithely along, straining out gnats and swallowing camels.

STRAINING OUT GNATS AND SWALLOWING CAMELS

In Matthew 23 Jesus warned his true spiritual followers about the hypocritical Pharisees, people who, Jesus said, "do not practice what they preach" (v. 3). Publicly and with great showiness the Pharisees and other teachers of the law tithed their income yet "neglected the more important matters of the law—justice, mercy and faithfulness" (v. 23). Concerning the Pharisees, Jesus told his followers, "Everything they do is done for men to see" (v. 5). Jesus said the Pharisees might be clean on the outside, but inside they were "full of greed and self-indulgence" (v. 25).

The Pharisees judged everyone else based on their own man-made code of conduct. This penchant for making up their own rules for spiritual behavior was so pronounced, and the Pharisees' consequent neglect of biblical principles so profound, that Jesus said, "You blind guides! You strain out a gnat but swallow a camel" (v. 24).

Straining out gnats and swallowing camels—that's the general condition of many Christians and churches in this postmodern culture. They're not operating with a spiritually discerning, Christian worldview. They've forgotten about, never understood, or rarely applied Christian liberty. In their effort to be not of the world, they've simply become "otherworldly," focusing on minor matters and therefore having very little or no earthly impact.

When Christians worry about the cultural gnats in their environment, they miss some of the much more spiritually threatening camels. For example, Christians break fellowship with other believers over the color of carpet in the church (this is not an apocryphal illustration but has really happened in many churches) or whether hymnbooks are used in the service, while they fail to challenge local schools, universities, and zoos that teach evolutionary theory.

Christians argue and split congregations over the use of drums or guitars in the church, while the philosophic implications of the use of technology of any kind are largely ignored. Often Christians react angrily when a young person gets a tattoo or wears a ring in an eyebrow, while Christian moral outrage is at best limited in the face of America's seduction by legalized commercial gambling.[4]

Christians are good at straining out gnats, and, like the insect, there are seemingly an unlimited number of gnat-like issues. But two gnats occupy more of our attention than any others: music styles and fads or fashions.

Music: The Number One Gnat

Music seems to be the number one gnat on which Christians focus. While music clearly offers legitimate grounds for Christian liberty debates and sanctified disagreements, music can nevertheless be a gnat that causes us to miss the more spiritually threatening camels. For example, is the person who makes the following observation a cynic or a realist? Consider these words: "American Christians dispute the type of music appropriate for worship while church members gossip, lie, and generally ignore premarital sex and adultery between its members."[5] These are fairly harsh words, but honesty requires us to admit that they're an all too accurate description of many churches. We strain at gnats and swallow camels.

Music is a cultural battleground. No other issue causes more church division than Christian culture wars fought over music. No other issue demonstrates more clearly that Christian liberty may be the least understood and least practiced doctrine in the Bible. No other issue better illustrates (or more wrenchingly illustrates) Christians' lack of a fully developed Christian worldview.

A Christian worldview informs us: "The world as created is an unfinished symphony. God called man, his cultural creature and co-worker, to take up the work and bring it to the fullness of that perfection which God had placed in it as promise."[6] Music is part of that unfinished symphony. Christians need to understand music in terms of the biblical definition of life, provided by a Christian worldview.

Music is a fine art, and as a fine art it is forever changing—and changing rapidly. That's because music, like all artistic expression, captures as much emotion as reason. It seeks to express thoughts that are as yet inexpressible in a more detailed and analytic form.

I don't mean that music isn't rational. Indeed, music is capable of incredible statements of deeply thought-out philosophy, ordered and harmonic, dissonant and noisy. But the special gift of music is that it is affective. It appeals to our innermost feelings. Consequently, people's taste in music is highly personal, preferential, and idiosyncratic. We know what we like and like what we know. We like what we like whether others like it or not.

In times of rapid social change, some music is always on the frontier of discussion and development. So if you like today's music, you may not like tomorrow's, because you may not share the values, feelings, and philosophies being expressed. Then again, if you don't like today's music, be patient until tomorrow, and, like the weather, another style of music will develop.

Music is preference. It's preferential because it's so personal. In any given family, spouses and other family members may have very different musical tastes. So judging what is good or bad in music is forever problematic. As with all questions in life, the key to determining acceptability for the Christian is whether the music directly violates Scripture or whether the music falls within the infinite realm of choice that God has given us. If it does not undermine clearly stated spiritual principles of Scripture, then the music must not be labeled bad in the sense of non-Christian or nonspiritual. On the other hand, music may be judged Christian and spiritual yet be considered qualitatively inferior musically, whether we like it or not.

Music is a universal language. Music enables us to communicate across time, across cultures, and across psychological and geographic space. Music may be a philosophic statement or an emotional expression, deep or shallow, profound or simple. As such, it is a language within language. If the music doesn't violate Scripture, Christians should be able to appreciate the variety of humanity's God-given musical gifts, even if we do not like or prefer certain styles.

Christians ought to be able to listen to different kinds of musical styles and lyrical content and determine what the writers and/or performers are trying to say to the world. What is the country artist saying, or the rapper, or the rocker? For that matter, what is the contemporary Christian artist trying to say? Is one musical artist consistently immoral? Is another artist gifted at conveying the beauty of love and commitment? Is an entire genre of music biblically inappropriate? Or do some songs within the genre defy biblical principle while other songs do not? Are some songs within the genre harmless entertainment or a celebration of life or culture, which are important and enjoyable reminders of God-given blessings in his creation?

Music is a means of communication. It can be Christian, non-Christian, or anti-Christian. Whatever it is, Christians who care about influencing their culture for Christ need to learn to speak the language. What is our teenagers' music saying? Is it all bad, or is at least some of it silly but harmless? Yes, it's true that today's songs are sometimes musically immature, even primitive or juvenile. But whether or not we like it, our teenagers' music is a language that is communicating questions we need to hear and answer.

Music is a fine art, a preference, and a universal language. Because philosophic values, time, place, culture, event, and individual mood can all cause variations in it, music is highly idiosyncratic. Ten people will probably have ten different music tastes and expressions. As such, music has become the focal point of enormous emotional and spiritual energy, a genuine battleground for many Christian people.

Here's a reminder and a caveat. This discussion should not be read as a blanket approval of all forms and styles of music. That is not what a Christian worldview demands of us. We must think and act biblically. Music is a gnat not because it does not matter or because every musical expression should be endorsed. Music is a gnat in the Christian community because we fight about it on levels of preference better left to Christian liberty rather than on worldview levels demanding a discerning response.

Music is a mirror to the soul. Music, like every other gift of God, has been and is being perverted by the sinful heart of humanity. "Show me the songs that a nation sings and I will forecast the moral future of that nation." [7] We cannot separate our aesthetics from our ethics.

So our attitude toward and opinion of certain kinds of music or specific music expressions, like all the arts, must be spiritually discerned on the basis of biblical principle and Christian liberty. Music not only can but should be discussed or debated in the church, but music should not divide the church. Informed discussion and even debate is an appropriate product of the Cultural Mandate. Division is a product of sin and a tool of Satan.

The Fickle Fate of Fads and Fashions

Christian culture wars are fought over a nearly infinite variety of issues. It seems that our ability to create our own holy lists knows no limit. One more of these cultural issues significantly and perennially disrupts Christian unity and therefore demands our attention—clothing and fashion fads. As an obstacle in our mission to fulfill the Cultural Mandate and the Great Commission, fashion styles rank near music in importance. Given the amount of emotional and spiritual energy we pour into the debate, I'd have to say that fashion fads are another gnat.

Let me illustrate. A few years ago a nationally known preacher spoke at Cornerstone University. During the chapel message, he vigorously derided former NBA rebounding star Dennis Rodman for the constantly varying unnatural colors of his hair. At the time, there were two students attending the university who wore their hair in bright, unnatural, sometimes fluorescent colors. I saw them in the balcony during that chapel and wondered what was going through their minds. These two young men were living dedicated Christian lives and playfully enjoyed their differently colored hair, which they did not associate with unbiblical attitudes and values. Today they wear their hair in their natural colors.

During the next week's chapels, I took what is a very rare step for our university and commented on this speaker's diatribe, noting the focus on Dennis Rodman's hair. My point with the students was that from a Christian point of view the color of Mr. Rodman's hair was the least spiritually objectionable thing about the man. His fame came more from his outrageous, degenerate behavior than from his basketball exploits. At the time, Mr. Rodman lived a highly public, in-your-face, immoral, even debauched lifestyle founded on a worldview antithetical to the Christian faith. The color of his hair, like the blue-colored hair of the elderly lady in church, simply does not mean much. It's a gnat.

Fads and fashions are notoriously fickle. During these postmodern times of rapid social change, clothing and personal appearance styles come and go, or more likely are simply layered, with astonishing speed. This fact alone should make Christians proceed with caution in creating bandwagons of resistance to fads and fashions. More to the point in terms of a Christian worldview, unless fads or fashions are immodest, we need to appreciate the variety and move on to more important concerns.

Modesty is the key biblical principle governing clothing choices. When Adam and Eve sinned against God in the Garden of Eden and knew that they were naked, they sewed fig leaves together and covered themselves. Later, after God had dealt with their sin, he made garments of skin and clothed them (Gen. 3:7, 21). How extensive these coverings were, we do not know. We do know that regardless of the culture in which we live and whatever the clothing styles of the moment, we are to dress modestly.

Beyond modesty, the Scripture does not give us any law; it gives us liberty. We are responsible to spiritually discern how to participate in fads and fashions in a manner that allows us to live in the world while being not of the world.

As with any perennial cultural question, simple rules of thumb don't work. Even my statement about modesty demands a corollary. Yes, modesty is the key to making biblically defensible decisions about clothing or personal appearance decisions, but clothing and other fashion accessories can become identified with a particular set of values, philosophic outlook or statement, or even an entire group or nation of people. Clothing is a part of cultural expression, so even modesty can at times be defined differently among Christians in different cultures.[8]

Clothing is a language, expressing some aspect of our worldview. Since clothing is a language, Christians must learn the language and discern whether they should be speaking it. And here's the corollary: This is true whether or not the clothing is modest. For example, traditional Amish clothing generally is very modest.[9] There is nothing intrinsically wrong with what Amish people typically wear, and they should enjoy every liberty to wear it. The same can be said for Orthodox Jews. But if you're not Amish or an Orthodox Jew, do you want to identify with their statement of values by wearing their style of clothing? Do you want your clothing to say something about you that may not be true?

It's possible to fulfill the basic biblical principle of modesty while creating certain standards of dress or personal appearance around a particular set of values. There's nothing inherently or biblically wrong with this. Jesus and his disciples dressed in the styles of their culture, a style quite different from what you might see in a typical American church in our postmodern times. Everyone lives in the world—in a culture—so we dress in a manner befitting that culture.

It's also possible to fulfill the basic biblical principle of modesty while creating fashion standards representing a set of values and a worldview with which Christians wish to disagree. For example, people who embrace Gothic music styles adopt dress and personal appearance styles that differ from the fashions of the biker group Hells Angels. Men or women involved in homosexuality sometimes dress in clothing and fashions that readily identify them as gay. American Nazi groups—Skinheads—are recognizable for their shaved heads and heavily tattooed bodies. American Hare Krishnas dress alike yet differently from those who dress for participation in witch covens or KKK rallies.

These are somewhat extreme examples, and I do not mean to equate the groups mentioned in this illustration in any way. They are distinct, even if sometimes overlapping in individual cases. Rather, I'm asking whether Christians really want to wear the clothing these groups wear—even if it's modest—and thus identify philosophically with the group's values. Therein lies my point. Sometimes we may choose to forgo a clothing style for a period of time, for while the style may not be evil in itself, it has become identified with a set of values we consider at odds with the Christian faith.

The same point may be made about clothing common to many American families. We need to think about what we're wearing. Are we modest? Are we consistently Christian in our choice of clothing? What about, for example, Christians wearing, or allowing their children to wear, clothes bearing conspicuous name brand labels or slogans? Do Americans, especially kids, own any clothing without labels or slogans? I'm not suggesting there's anything intrinsically evil about clothing labels, and I am a supporter of free enterprise. But as a way of illustrating Christian worldview thinking, I'm asking whether Christian people should be walking billboards. Are we harmlessly identifying with a favorite product or brand, or are we promoting conspicuous consumption or materialism? There it is, a subtly expressed value—conspicuous consumption. The clothing may be modest. The wording on the shirt may not be evil, but the values being expressed may still be biblically suspect. Promotion of a favorite brand or product is one thing; promotion of materialism is another. What's a Christian to do?

Christians, as always, are called to testify. Are we testifying for Christ or for cultural idols? Do we adorn ourselves with fads and fashions that represent harmless change, or do we adopt the latest style with little or no regard for whether it reinforces biblical modesty or proclaims values or even an entire worldview contrary to the Christian faith?

Clothing fads and fashions are subject to tradition and change, and they're highly visible for all to see. So clothing fads and fashions must be part of Christian reflection on living in the world while not of the world. It's not only okay to talk about clothing fads and fashions, we *should* talk about them.

Insofar as clothing fads and fashions are modest and otherwise unidentified with non-Christian philosophies, these fads and fashions should be the province of Christian liberty. Time and again, we spiritualize our taste and preference, turning them into cultural battlegrounds, and misspend far too much emotional and spiritual energy on this gnat. It's a big gnat, but it's still a gnat.

As long as Christians remain ignorant of the fact that clothing fads and fashions (or music) are a language, we will wear whatever is in, skipping right past the gnat and potentially swallowing a camel. Our Christian worldview both requires and prepares us to consider the values expressed in fads and fashions. The language of fads and fashions is sometimes subtle and demands a mature spiritual discernment, but learning to read or listen to this language is a necessary part of avoiding being conformed to this world.

WE'VE NEVER DONE IT THAT WAY

Tradition and change—in music, fashions, and a host of other cultural practices—exist side by side in postmodern culture. For Christians wishing to fulfill their biblical calling, this fact is one more minefield in the Christian culture wars. While the Scripture both embraces and criticizes varying traditions, the Christian church all too frequently resists any change in the name of "We've never done it that way." This does not mean that all traditions are bad or that all change is good. It does mean that Christians need to look at tradition and change with spiritually discerning eyes, keeping our Christian world-view in mind. Derek Tidball agrees:

> In holding firm we must hold firm to principles and revealed truths, not to forms, traditions, and structures which are vehicles that conveniently or aptly express those principles in any one age. Constantly the church needs to go back to the self-critical and painful task of asking itself what are its goals and aims and it needs to bring its structures and programmes into line with those aims.[10]

We know that some traditions add meaning, memory, and continuity to our lives and are harmless and enjoyable, for example, liturgies, annual Sunday school picnics, "In Remembrance of Me" tables at the front of the church, missionary flags of the nations hung in the narthex, organs on the left, pianos on the right, Sunday morning pastoral prayers, dressing up for Easter Sunday, and so on.

But some traditions become forms of meaningless ritual or legalism, preventing us from influencing contemporary culture. These include sectarianism, churchianity, the recitation of prayers from memory and not the heart, mandated fashion codes, restrictions on some musical instruments in church, and holy lists. It's this type of tradition that prompted Francis A. Schaeffer to observe, "The evangelical church seems to specialize in being behind."[11]

We must ask, Do we trust God alone? Is our sufficiency in Christ? Or do we trust God plus observances, laws, traditions, and practices? The latter position makes trust in God dependent on observances of customs.[12] Legalism in this form is a type of works-based salvation and as such drives a stake through the very heart of evangelical, biblical soteriology. Legalism is not just an unnecessary addition; it is sin.

Of course, some change is harmless, interesting, and perhaps a beneficial consequence of God-given creativity—for example most fads and fashions; many medical, scientific, and technological advances; new music and art forms; economic productivity based on human craftsmanship; and new forms of transportation. Different cultures exist because of this kind of change, which we may embrace.

Yet because of the evil nature of human beings, some change violates God's moral will. Christians should resist this kind of change, which includes sexual deviancy; moral relativism; some fads and fashions; abortion; the drug culture; some medical, scientific, and technological changes; and some new music and art.

Finally, there are still other changes that Christians should promote because they reform or transform culture in a manner consistent with biblical values. A good example of this kind of change is William Wilberforce's success in abolishing slavery in England. Other examples are the work of pro-life and anti-racism movements; spiritual awakenings leading to Christian evangelism and revival; prison reform; Christian expression in the arts, literature, and cinema; and Christian impact on politics, government, law, education, and other professions.

Christians must develop the wisdom to discern between rational and irrational tradition and responsible and irresponsible change. Francis A. Schaeffer put it this way:

> The church has a place but not if it ossifies. I think too often we are killing ourselves. We fail to distinguish the things that are open to change from those that are not. We must make ourselves available to the existential leading of the Holy Spirit. . . . Refusal to consider change under the direction of the Holy Spirit is a spiritual problem, not an intellectual problem.[13]

Change is not the Christian's enemy any more than tradition is always the Christian's friend. By the same token, change is not always the Christian's friend, nor is tradition always the enemy. The "enemy" is an uncritical acceptance of either tradition or change, an unexamined life governed by cultural convention and not Christian convictions.

Billy Graham's first crusade slogan was "Geared to the Times, Anchored to the Rock."[14] This may be marketing, but it's good theology too. Biblical Christianity is forever relevant and temporally applicable. Only enculturated Christians get out of date.

~~Surviving~~ Thriving in the Culture Wars

As I've repeatedly observed, the inability of Christians to deal with social change, and our penchant for robbing each other of divinely appointed Christian liberty, stymies our Christian witness. Our lack of a Christian worldview understanding about who God is results in weak spiritual discernment and therefore an ineffective impact on both culture and individuals.

Music and fashions are only two of the battlegrounds in the Christian culture wars. There are many others. The degree to which Christians succumb to these micro battles of their own culture wars is the degree to which they will not be fulfilled spiritually, because they will be accomplishing neither the Cultural Mandate nor the Great Commission.

Gnats and camels do not make a spiritually nourishing diet. A spiritually healthy diet comes through discernment and an effort to test everything against the teachings of God's Word. We need to do more than just survive the culture wars. We need to thrive by rising above them. Thriving is a matter of understanding that "to obey is better than sacrifice" (1 Sam. 15:22). God is not interested in conformity to a static code but to a person, the "likeness of his Son" (Rom. 8:29).[15] God gave us a biblical foundation for life and the Christian liberty to live it. Only by avoiding the micro battles of the culture wars can we hope to fight effectively the macro worldview battles facing postmodern culture.

The Christian life is about going "on to maturity" (Heb. 6:1). To thrive spiritually in the face of Christian culture wars, we must develop our theological understanding of social change. We also must learn to be discerning in the context of a biblically Christian worldview and rediscover Christian liberty.

9

CHRISTIANS IN A POMO CULTURE

"Love your neighbor as yourself." Love does no harm to its neighbor. Therefore love is the fulfillment of the law. And do this, understanding the present time. The hour has come for you to wake up from your slumber, because our salvation is nearer now than when we first believed.

Romans 13:9–11

As we've learned thus far, early twenty-first-century life is characterized by rapid, uncertain, and chaotic social and cultural change. It's a time when many people, including many Christians, are experiencing a crisis of confidence, not only because they don't know what's going to happen but also because they don't know what to think about what's going to happen. With a postmodern mentality dominating current culture, there is an irrationalism in society that invites, if not celebrates, a crisis of confidence in what we believe.

CHRISTIAN CONFIDENCE

Christian people, of course, are very much a part of these changing times. That's why I think it's a bit ironic if not amusing when people say that Christians should get involved. This comment misses the point. We *are* involved. We're in the world. To use a double negative, we can't *not* be in the world. We're part of the culture, society, and age in which we live. These are our times. And whether we know it or not, whether we like it or not, we're influenced by the postmodern mentality's attitudes, goals, and evaluation of our religious beliefs—and for that matter everything else in our lives.

But Christians are supposed to be different. We're God's remnant, his ambassadors. As representatives of a timeless faith, we're not supposed to kowtow to time-bound assumptions, attitudes, and actions. We're not supposed to adopt a postmodern mentality and certainly not a worldview characterized by the tenets of postmodernism. We're constrained to rise above these influences and act as influencers of the world around us. That's what the Cultural Mandate, the Great Commission, and the New Testament concepts of salt and light are all about. Through them God commissions Christians to

> develop culture;
> go and teach all people about Christ and Christianity;
> help define and direct the culture in which we live;
> lead others to reconciliation with God through Christ.

Without this Christian witness, culture is doomed to an untempered course designed by the deceitful human heart and the finite human mind. Without this Christian witness, individuals alienated from God by sinful hearts are left to a problem without remedy.

Actually, Christian confidence should be high, even in the face of extensive social change and associated human problems, for we know something about the remedy.

THE POSTMODERN PREDICAMENT

The new postmodern mentality now affects not just *what* people think but *how* they think. This is where the impact of nonbiblical perspectives can be so subtle and so powerful at the same time.

In the postmodern mentality, the ideas of choice or process matter more than results. While the modern mentality embraced reality, substance, rationale, content, and facts, the postmodern mentality travels an entirely different path, celebrating illusion, image, the sound bite, intuition, impressions, and style. Even people's image of God changes. The postmodern mentality leaves room for God to exist, but he's limited to my conception or yours of what he can do. In other words, he's made in our image rather than the other way around. This lesser God is not sovereign, omniscient, or omnipotent. He's just a nice concept, sort of like a teddy bear, warm and fuzzy, there when you need him but otherwise not relevant to your life.

In this way the postmodern mentality creates a predicament for itself that it cannot fix. With no transcendent, sovereign God, and therefore no concept of absolute or objective truth, people are "free" to think subjectively and intuitively. Now set loose from what God says is objectively real and true and worthy, people pursue their own answers. Inevitably and unavoidably (because we are inescapably religious creatures), people turn to a Pandora's box of false and limited spiritualities. God becomes god and people simply do what is right in their own eyes.

The postmodern mentality—the new approach affecting *how* people think as well as *what* they think—is evident in every human endeavor. In politics, a declining acknowledgment of ultimate truths produces a political climate in which it becomes more important who or what group said something than whether what was said is verifiably true. This point was on display during both the infamous 1990s O. J. Simpson trial and President Bill Clinton's impeachment process. Power and pretense more often than principle fuel the political engines of postmodern culture.

In art, timeless virtues like beauty, excellence, or logic are set aside in favor of vulgarity, randomness, banality, superficiality, dehumanization, or power agendas, with few aesthetic standards left that are capable of distinguishing art from pornography or obscenity. Not all art, of course, displays these characteristics, but you can easily discover what I mean by taking a walk through the postmodern art section of your local art museum. You'll find far more evidence of disharmony and despair than of harmony and happiness.

Literature, drama, and the cinema are dominated by PoMo themes: prurient interest and cheap titillation; text with no meaning; plotless novels and films; immorality; antiheroes who use illegal means to accomplish ostensibly "good" ends; gratuitous, even random and nonsensical violence; and certainly a generalized dumbing down and vulgarization of content. Again, like art, not all writing is like this, but it is increasingly difficult to find new authors who are not pandering to the baser tastes of postmodern culture.

In higher education, the postmodern mentality welcomes virtually any worldview except Christianity, which is considered intolerant because of its affirmation of moral absolutes. Students' values—whether modern, postmodern, or otherwise—are frequently deconstructed, with no values but moral relativism and maybe egalitarianism put in their place. While I hasten to note that many moral and decent people (including Christians) work in the nation's universities, I can still defend my observation that in the vast majority of schools, no intentional, campuswide moral philosophy for how to use knowledge is provided. This is so because many universities, which still say their purpose is a search for truth, employ many faculty members who no longer believe in truth. The reality is that universities support a search for information that yields image and stature, for these are commodities Postmodernity recognizes.

The postmodern mentality promotes "freedom" of the mind and the spirit from moral absolutes yet in the end enslaves itself to whatever is in vogue. This is Postmodernity's own cultural contradiction, its own predicament. Moreover, the postmodern predicament is a paradox—the more postmodern culture ostensibly maximizes freedom *through* moral relativism, the more it actually minimizes freedom *by* moral relativism.

Postmodern culture wants freedom without the Spirit who makes it possible. The PoMo mentality wants spirits without the Spirit. It is a false religion, one producing many "unfreedoms," the faux freedoms of promiscuity, disease, emotional and physical pain, addiction, dissipation, and anomie. The assumption that moral relativism sets postmodern culture free ultimately makes it less free, because now the mind and spirit are given over to current whims or individual opinion with no means of determining what is true, good, healthy, fulfilling, or worthwhile. But we can be thankful that the story does not end here.

CHALLENGING CHANGE

The paradox of the postmodern predicament opens the door to individual and cultural witness. Our sovereign Creator God is still in control, and he is giving Christians a new and great spiritual opportunity to fulfill the Cultural Mandate and the Great Commission. The postmodern predicament reintroduces an old problem. It makes the meaning of our existence problematic, and consequently, the fundamental frailty of the human condition is laid bare.[1] The more thoroughly and vigorously people embrace the moral relativism of the postmodern mentality, along with the vague superstitious spiritualism it produces, the more they lose touch with a trustworthy explanation of why human beings exist, what life is all about, and where human beings are headed. People no longer can find any reasonable and trustworthy (two ideas the postmodern mentality injects with uncertainty) answers to basic questions.

When I speak of challenging change, therefore, I'm suggesting both an explanation of the stresses of our times and a description of the calling we must pursue. Christians are agents of an eternal, living God and his revealed living truth. It's our responsibility to demonstrate—to live out—stability, reality, and hope in the midst of social change. Also, our responsibility before God is to be his change agents, working to alter any cultural development or expression that is counter to his will. It is exciting to realize that we have a great opportunity to show our neighbors what a different approach—a Christian approach—to life in these PoMo times looks like.

On an individual level, men and women influenced by a postmodern mentality need synthesis and stability in the face of confusion. They need explanations that work. "We need to address the postmoderns' existential predicament. It's tough living as a postmodern. It's tough living without certainty."[2] Our neighbors need to see that biblical truth-claims fit reality in a way that the ideological assumptions of other worldviews do not. People need focus. To put it plainly, whether or not they realize it, they need a raison d'être.

Christians who believe the Bible say we have truth. Therefore, because we believe that our faith is relevant to all aspects of life, this is an especially significant time for us. To fulfill God's commands in our own lives, we must be willing to wrestle with the vagaries of postmodern culture and attempt to develop our faith's perspective on postmodern issues.[3]

But we have an apparent inability to challenge change or to work productively with change that is challenging. We are so focused on the burdens of our lives, often falling down under the weight of them, that we are unable to assist nonbelieving neighbors in PoMo culture with their burdens. Charles Colson and Nancy Pearcey described our problem this way: "A debilitating weakness in modern evangelicalism is that we've been fighting cultural skirmishes on all sides without knowing what the war itself is about."[4] We're fighting each other in Christian culture wars, and we've joined our postmodern neighbors in fighting culture battles on innumerable, important, but, to our way of thinking, unconnected issues.

Christians need to recognize the worldview connection between seemingly unconnected cultural issues. Because PoMo culture no longer affirms an objective standard of truth, our most fundamental and cherished assumptions about how to order our lives are now at odds with the dominant paradigm of our own culture. Add to this the postmodern mentality's promotion of indeterminacy in all fact and value discussions, and you can see why PoMo culture has become a battleground for numberless distinctive-but-connected culture fights, including abortion, childcare, funding (and standards) for the arts, affirmative action and quotas, gay rights, values in public education, multiculturalism, and much more. These culture fights turn into social and political battles (different from the Christian culture wars being waged within our churches), which ultimately may be traced to the worldview issue of moral authority, meaning the basis by which people determine whether something is good or bad, right or wrong, acceptable or unacceptable.[5]

So Christians, already divided, confused, and weakened by the Christian culture wars within the church, join with or debate their postmodern neighbors in myriad political battles. Now the two great culture wars are intermingled, the micro culture war for the soul of the church and the macro culture war for the soul of the nation.

As this happens, Christians generally take one of two routes. One, we present an overconfident, triumphant, sometimes self-righteous attitude toward our nonbelieving neighbors, earning for ourselves derisive monikers like Fighting Fundies, Bible Thumpers, or Cultural Moralists. Some Christians embrace such names and proudly endure the name-calling, but labels are really beside the point. The real tragedy is not the verbal sticks and stones but the Christian witness that's diluted and the battle that's lost.

More often Christians present an underconfident, uncertain, disjointed, and sometimes confused attitude toward our nonbelieving neighbors' favored issues, making it fairly easy for the usually well-heeled, well-prepared, well-spoken opposition groups to defeat

Christian perspectives, to say nothing of the general public's ignoring us. What's the tragedy here? We lose an opportunity for spiritually and culturally constructive change for the glory of God.

When Christians engage in culture wars without the spiritual, intellectual, and philosophical armaments of a developed, biblical Christian worldview, they become just another fragmented community drifting along among many others. Consequently, the moral authority of Christians in the postmodern culture is truncated, damaged, and maybe silenced altogether. Christians lose culture battles not because biblical Christianity is weak, untrue, or irrelevant but because Christians are ill prepared to fight the good fight.

APPLYING SCRIPTURAL PRINCIPLES TO POMO TIMES

This is the time when the Christian church should shine. This is our chance to honor God's command to go into the world, but we must be prepared to do so. With the church's help, Christian people can learn to do moral reasoning on the issues of our day.

The church should be asking, as Brian McLaren does, "How does the Spirit of Jesus Christ incarnate in a postmodern world?"[6] Sermons should remind parishioners of the need for a right heart before God (which is critically important). But we can't stop there, as too many evangelical churches do. Sermons also should encourage Christians to convey to the society in which they live that Christ is Lord of all of life and culture. Sermons and services need to address everyday cultural issues directly, practically, and courageously. In other words, churches must help Christian people develop a thoroughly Christian worldview and understand how their worldview speaks to everyday culture. They also must help Christians see the worldview "connect" among current cultural debates.

When Christians fight in culture wars, either within the church or within the culture, without the benefit of a Christian worldview and without benefit of biblical spiritual discernment, they're like soldiers doing battle without command or communication. They're weakened by lack of direction, understanding, and coordination.

Churches should be sources of biblical understanding that can be readily and practically translated to contemporary concerns. Without the understanding, integration, confidence, and liberty provided by a biblical Christian worldview, Christians are incapable of presenting a philosophically united front. We don't understand our own belief system (biblical doctrine). We don't know how those beliefs apply to the challenges of our times. So we react to those challenges in a fractured, even contradictory, fashion. Why? Because we're all saluting the same Commander, but we're not all following his commands.

The Bible is neither a political manual nor a social tract. It is the will of the living God for the world he created. Our understanding of the Cultural Mandate demands that we apply scriptural principles to the issues of our times. The Great Commission demands that we take the gospel to our PoMo neighbors. Churches that arm their people with a Christian worldview will encourage their personal piety while avoiding conformity with the world but will also help to transform their minds for the worldview battles of current culture.

As we enter the spiritual and cultural warfare of our times, Christians must be able to recognize the degree to which our idea of Christianity has itself been unbiblically acculturated. Christians must consistently and consciously conduct a self-examination, using Scripture as a guide. And as much of this book has stressed, we also must examine our culture. If we do not understand our culture, we do not understand ourselves. If we do not understand Scripture, we do not understand how God sees us or how God expects us to interact with culture.

Basically, in our diverse and changing PoMo culture, all Christians need to think like missionaries—to think cross-culturally. For generations missionaries have been sent to far-off lands and have been expected to learn the language, learn the culture, become like the people they are trying to reach, stopping short of violating scriptural principles, and then share the gospel and apply the Word of God. Christians must do the same thing right here in our own culture. We must learn the culture and identify with the people we're trying to reach. Terry M. Crist puts it this way: "Effective cross-cultural communication of the Gospel is accomplished, first, by scraping away the barnacles of nonessential religious tradition that have attached themselves to us over time. In other words, eliminate the stuff that obscures the fundamental essence of Christianity in the minds of nonreligious people."[7]

Without this effort, we're left with an acculturated Christianity, a crippled and myopic Christianity. It's a sad Christianity that blends beyond recognition with its culture and is unable to provide necessary spiritual vitality. True Christianity transcends culture, depending for its vitality on the Word, an extension of the character and purpose of the Living Word. Christians understand that

> there is no cultureless gospel. Jesus himself preached, taught, and healed within a specific cultural context. Nor is it that the gospel can be reduced to a set of cultureless principles. . . . *One of the tasks of the church is to translate the gospel so that the surrounding culture can understand it, yet help those believers who have been in that culture move toward living according to the behaviors and communal identity of God's missional people.*[8]

A Christian worldview makes it possible to translate all biblical teaching for individual edification and cultural transformation. A Christian worldview enables us, for example, to distinguish between *personal* Christian morality and a biblically informed, *public* moral philosophy—to distinguish between sin and crime.[9] I am not advocating Christian control of government, but I am reminding us that not-of-the-world Christians are in the world and must also go into the world to fulfill God's will. We must apply our Christian worldview in culture, or we are disobedient to God.

This means speaking winsomely and intelligently to our non-Christian neighbors about issues that matter to them—as the apostle Paul did at Areopagus. Acts 17 tells us that Paul's spirit was greatly distressed because the city of Athens was "full of idols" (v. 16). Athens was the intellectual and cultural center of its day, and the city attracted learned people who did not know the one true God. Learned, without knowledge of the Truth, Athens was a place of sophisticated ignorance. So Paul responded with a two-pronged approach. He went to the synagogue—to the religious people—and then he reasoned in the marketplace "with those who happened to be there" (v. 17). He went to the "churched," and he went to the culture. He took the gospel to individuals to change them, and he gave them a Christian worldview capable of changing their culture.

The Christian church's challenge today is to keep reaching the churched and the unchurched but also to have an impact on the PoMo culture in which we live. Our opportunity is to share a Christian worldview that speaks to all of life, providing the way of individual salvation and the truth and life for cultural transformation.

Our message is of ultimate importance, but methods matter too. *How* we share a Christian worldview in PoMo culture is key to its impact.

A CHRISTIAN RESPONSE TO CATASTROPHIC CHANGE

On September 11, 2001, an Afghanistan-based terrorist group launched an unforgettable attack on America, which destroyed the World Trade Center in New York City, severely damaged the Pentagon in Washington, D.C., and caused a plane full of people to crash in Pennsylvania—terrorism on American soil. The aftermath of this unprovoked aggression has become a tragic but instructive case study on how PoMo culture might respond to catastrophic stress and change.

This particular demonstration of human depravity, live and in color, next door in America, literally shook people to the core of their spiritual beings. A terrorist arrow struck the Big Apple in a manner heretofore inconceivable. The twin icons of American capitalism—the World Trade Towers—were literally brought down. At least temporarily, American military might appeared ineffective. Thousands of innocents died. This was revolutionary, sudden social change, and because death is the ultimate undeniable reality, it wrenched people spiritually in a way this generation had never seen.

Even months later as I write this, the degree to which this attack and its repercussions will result in a spiritual and social sea change in American culture is something yet to be fully determined. But this horrific event does pose some compelling questions about spiritual and social change: In the face of tragedy, will Americans turn to biblical Christianity, or will they react in a more postmodern fashion, grasping for answers in the vogue but vague spiritualism of our times? And how can Christians respond to an event like 9/11 in a manner that will point nonbelieving neighbors to Jesus Christ and biblical Christianity?

Clearly God can use tragedy and the openness in hearts it typically produces to bring about an awakening of interest in Christ and Christianity. This has happened before in human history, and no biblical reason exists for it not to happen again. As anyone who lived through this period will recall, people the world over immediately began searching for meaning. On television *God* became a name once again, not just a curse word. National newscasters and politicians began using words like *evil, moral,* even *sin.* The Bible was read at length in service after service broadcast around the world. Christianity, systematically ignored by the dominant culture and media in the decades and days prior to the attack, began ringing loud and clear through the voices of survivors or their loved ones. So in the wake of sudden death and change, the truth of biblical Christianity, along with many other expressions of religious hope, was proclaimed.

But the questions still remain: Will people turn to the Truth, or will people follow the morally relativistic notions of postmodern culture, patching together their own answers—creating their own meaning?

As we've learned, the name of the game in postmodern culture, religiously speaking, is syncretism. People don't *receive and believe* their religious convictions. They *build* their religious convictions, one belief at a time, a little bit of this and a little bit of that. In this postmodern mode, people want spirituality but are not at all concerned that one tenet of their faith may be contradictory to another. What matters to many people is that they have faith (in whatever) and their religious views work for them.

In the aftermath of the terrorist attack of September 11, 2001, people have responded spiritually in two ways. Some have turned to the infinite and living God of biblical Christianity, and many have turned to the finite gods of counterfeit faiths.

How PoMo culture develops from this point in time, only God knows. But some important observations can be made for Christians wishing to fulfill their spiritual responsibility and opportunity in this Christ-starved culture.

The "This Is That" Fallacy

Christians have a tendency to claim an "insider" knowledge about God's purposes on earth by saying, "God is doing this," or "God is doing that." It's what Francis A. Schaeffer called the "this is that" fallacy, our inclination to say, "This event in our time is the fulfillment of that prophecy in the Bible."[10] Many Christians make the mistake of proclaiming they have a hotline to God that allows them to speak *ex cathedra* (as a religious authority) or *vox Dei* (with the voice of God). This is not only inaccurate, it is sin.

Christians do not possess, nor do they need, detailed explanations for divine activity. Remember Romans 11:33–34: "Oh, the depth of the riches of the wisdom and knowledge of God! How unsearchable his judgments, and his paths beyond tracing out! Who has known the mind of the Lord? Or who has been his counselor?" We do know who God is, and we know his character. Consequently, we should remind our friends, Christians and non-Christians alike, that God is the great and majestic God, omniscient, merciful, just, and holy.

The Power of the Word

Christians should rejoice when the Bible is presented, even when it is shared by someone who espouses religious views contrary to our own. Not everyone affirms a biblically Christian position, but the Bible is God's Word. He has told us that it will not return to him empty but will accomplish his desires and achieve the purpose for which he revealed it (Isa. 55:11). Remember Philippians 1:18: "But what does it matter? The important thing is that in every way, whether from false motives or true, Christ is preached. And because of this I rejoice."

Speaking Out about Faith

Christians should be prepared to speak intelligently and enthusiastically about their faith. Our postmodern neighbors will never hear the truth of the gospel if we do not live it and share it. Human tragedy and the social changes that may result from it should not catch us spiritually unaware. In terrible times, our non-Christian neighbors should see real faith and genuine hope in us, not frantic fear. Remember 1 Peter 3:15: "But in your hearts set apart Christ as Lord. Always be prepared to give an answer to everyone who asks you to give the reason for the hope that you have. But do this with gentleness and respect."

Our Christian worldview and our understanding of what God says about social change and history provide us with the principles people need in times of great distress. We realize that no one knows the future except God, and we believe that God is in sovereign control of history, even catastrophic events. So our Christian response should not be to worry about the details of emerging history as much as to evidence trust in the God of history.

How we evidence our faith in times of crisis is immensely important. Telling people, "This is what the Lord God says . . ." and sharing pointed criticism and little else is not necessarily the best approach. In 1 Peter 3:15 the apostle instructs us to speak with "gentleness and respect." We are expected to give people a "reason for the hope" but always with "gentleness and respect." We must show searching, sometimes hurting people Christ's love. Then show them his truth. If we do not first show them love, they may not be able to see or hear the truth. The truth may be lost in the fog of their confusion and their hurt. Particularly in postmodern culture, when people do not believe much of anything is real, sharing an authentic love is a first step to renewal. A culture's spiritual sea change begins with one changed heart.

The postmodern predicament and the challenging changes (including especially catastrophic events) of this age leave people with a vitiated hope. Rootless and centerless, our postmodern neighbors literally do not know where to turn.

CHRISTIAN HOPE IN A HOPELESS WORLD

Hope springs eternal in the human heart, but where is hope in a hopeless postmodern world? PoMo hope is like PoMo truth, illusory and subjective. So PoMo hope is really not hope, for hope that has no basis is at best a temporary opiate, just a mask for quiet desperation.

A hope is only as good as its foundation or focus. Christian hope—a confident expectation of fulfillment—is based on an objective source of divine personality, strength, and power in Jesus Christ. It is not, therefore, a vain, irrationally conceived, frivolous human wish but a rational confidence in something real. Christian hope rests on truth revealed in Christ, truth experienced in the Christian life, and truth expected in the coming of Christ's kingdom.

Christian hope operates between the extremes of utopianism on the one hand and fatalism on the other. Modernity's mentality was dominated by naturalistic humanism, optimistically espousing permanent growth and well-being in a secular leap of faith. Postmodernity, on the other hand, exhibits a new desperate, if not nihilistic, mentality that is uncertain about the future, technology, or life itself. The modern mentality dreamed of progress. The postmodern mentality has given way to pessimism, even panic. Neither Mod nor PoMo culture has an answer for death. Christian hope rejects the positions of both the modern and postmodern mentalities as unwarranted and unbiblical extremes.

In the words of a popular Christian song, "Because Christ lives, we can face tomorrow." Our hope is grounded in a person of the Godhead and in already accomplished historical events—Jesus' death, burial, and resurrection. The promise of our deliverance in time and our ultimate reconciliation with Christ in heaven is sure. We can believe, and therefore we can have hope.

Certainly a Christian can be neither an unqualified optimist nor an unqualified pessimist. Philosophic humanists generally embrace one extreme or the other, because they have no basis, as Christians do, for intellectually assimilating both good and evil. Christians should be optimistic, though not with the irrational faith of the evolutionary theorist or the blind faith of modern culture in the idea of progress. We can be optimistic, because we know that ultimately God will have his way in the world. No Christian, however, should ever be a pessimist. Pessimism is reserved for those who have no hope.

A Christian's optimism must be tempered by realism.[11] We must not forget that the world and humanity are fallen and cursed; evil continues, abated only by the restraining power of the Holy Spirit and God's common grace; and all of us are sinners in need of redemption. Realism serves as a warning against temptations to triumphalism.[12] Humility, not bravado, must characterize the Christian's hope. Therefore Christians should be both optimistic and realistic, or optimistic realists.

As optimistic realists with a well-developed Christian worldview, Christians should evidence humble hope and confidence in a culture that no longer believes either one is possible. If we do this, our lives become books with a message our neighbors can read, books that point them to the way, the truth, and the life.

In the words of John Jay more than two centuries ago, we live "in times which [try] the minds and hearts of men."[13] We live in a time when culture is chasing the wind. But it is the Lord Christ we are serving, and he says to the wind, "Peace be still." Social change, comprehensive or catastrophic, minute or mundane, is in the hands of God. That's our witness to PoMo culture.

10

MAKING THE MOST OF EVERY OPPORTUNITY

Be very careful, then, how you live—not as unwise but as wise, making the most of every opportunity, because the days are evil.

Ephesians 5:15–16

Running around saying the sky is falling with no suggestion of how to stop it is not very helpful. But a lot of Christians are like this. We know something is wrong with the world, and we've even cared for the root of the problem in our own lives through individual salvation by faith in Christ, but we're not really sure what to do about the problem in the culture around us. And worse, many of us sell our souls to the defense of selected cultural practices, what we consider *the* Christian way of doing things, and this doesn't stop the sky from falling either.

Contemporary postmodern culture is in even worse shape than the Christian subculture entwined in culture wars. For our culture, the sky *is* falling, so to speak, and a lot of people are running around talking about it. The pundits of the day give us many solutions for fixing our world, but then there's another problem—no one seems to believe any of the solutions will really work.

Of all people, Christians should *know* the sky is falling. But we should be the last ones running around without a remedy. Yet we are. Time and again we fail to act like contemporary "men and women of Issachar," who not only know the times but know what we ought to do.

We don't *act* confidently because we haven't *thought* confidently. Because our Christian worldview understanding of our faith is deficient, we don't act like we're "more than conquerors through him who loved us" or like we believe that "neither the present nor the future" can "separate us from the love of God that is in Christ Jesus our Lord" (Rom. 8:37–39). Too often we're not so much *conquerors* of change as *casualties* of change.

I've talked a lot about social change in this book because change is a part of life and this world. Christians, who are charged with stewarding both our lives and the world, must therefore understand social change, how to interact with it, how to evaluate it, how to embrace or resist it, how to transform it, and how to create it.

Change is a fundamental characteristic of the wonderful world God created and is therefore a gift from God. Like all gifts from God, social change is often perverted by human sin, but this fact doesn't alter the essential goodness of the gift. Creation is God's garden and we are his gardeners, his stewards, both commanded and invited to experience all that he places in the garden. This includes change as well as order.

God's Word tells us what we need to know about his world. The greater our understanding and application of the biblical message, the greater will be our ability to holistically—spiritually, intellectually, emotionally, and physically—engage and enjoy creation and image God's deity by creating culture. As we engage and enjoy creation the way God intended and as we develop God-glorifying culture, we become more fully human.[1]

To be fully human, fully Christian, is to be holistically liberated. Christians who understand the Christian worldview of their faith are liberated from fear of social change. They're liberated from the inevitability of cultural captivity. They're liberated to enjoy God's creation and all of life. They are liberated to fulfill the Cultural Mandate and the Great Commission. They're liberated to share the reconciling good news of Jesus Christ, seeing people redeemed and culture transformed.

CHRISTIAN CULTURAL CONUNDRUMS

We've said that the single greatest obstacle to the Christian church's fulfillment of the Cultural Mandate and the accomplishment of the

Great Commission is its inability to deal with social change. The church is missing a spiritually discerning Christian worldview capable of informing its attitudes and activities in the face of challenging change. So rapid change overwhelms us, and we tend to withdraw into philosophic if not geographic protected zones, limiting our impact on culture.

Floundering without Discernment

Without a developed Christian worldview, we flounder, not knowing how to deal with the "in the world/not of the world tension." Without the spiritual discernment that comes from a developed Christian worldview, we can't answer crucial questions like, "One, how far can the church go in order to become relevant and meet the demands of the age, and two, how strong are the defenses of the church against the encroachments of the world outside?"[2] We can't answer these questions because we haven't used the wisdom tools God has given us.

Ignoring Christian Liberty

The church struggles in part because it ignores Christian liberty. As a result, the church manufactures its own culture wars. The church institutionalizes its values, emotions, and organizational structures into routines, and these routines become "sacred."[3] In other words, the church weds itself to selected cultural forms and methods. This reduces the joys of Christian fellowship even as it reinforces the church's social distance from contemporary culture. Eventually the church can fall into legalism, producing fear and frustration—or maybe, even worse, irrelevance. In this way, the church never knows the joy of liberty grounded in truth, and the end result is a church that's more reactive than proactive. Meanwhile, individual Christians become more confused, conflicted, and lacking in confidence to engage the changing culture in which they live.

Without a developed Christian worldview, Christians are left without answers and without defenses. Many Christians evidence no more depth of moral reasoning than what's regularly seen on bumper stickers. They're saved, but they're not serving. They own a Bible, but they don't know how to apply its principles either on the home

front or in the marketplace. This is both curious and sad, because
Christians know that where the Spirit of the Lord is, there is freedom—the world's greatest cause. Yet theologically, philosophically,
intellectually, and spiritually, we're unprepared to address the moral
chaos of contemporary postmodern culture.

Embracing instead of Critiquing Culture

Christians who fail to develop a Christian worldview are unable
to critique their culture, and thus they inevitably embrace it. When
it comes to the "in the world/not of the world tension," they lose
by default, having never wrestled with the truth. They simply accommodate the culture, embracing one version or another of churchianity. Christians who identify their faith with cultural practices tend
to develop their own factions or interest groups, little different from
the culture around them. Though Christians are given *unity* in the
Spirit through obedience to God's Word, they create *disunity* instead.
Therefore Christians appear just as confused as the chaotic culture
in which they live.

Certainly Christians need to understand that "history makes culture religionists look a little silly."[4] If you identify your faith with
time-bound cultural practices or methods, very soon your presumed
relevance will become irrelevance. Times change, and Christians
who cannot understand change undermine their own ability to
address the questions and issues of emerging culture. When this happens, the church first becomes more inward focused or privatized;
then, in terms of the broader culture, the church becomes less consequential or is marginalized. The result is a church prevented by
its irrelevance to the culture from providing a coherent voice of
truth amid cultural confusion. Yet we really aren't "prevented" from
influencing culture at all; we've done it to ourselves; we've made
ourselves irrelevant.

The Scripture tells us, "Faith comes from hearing the message"
(Rom. 10:17). And again, "How can they believe in the one of whom
they have not heard? And how can they hear without someone
preaching to them?" (v. 14). If the church doesn't speak the Word of
God into culture, nonbelievers may not hear it, and if they don't hear
it, they can't come to faith in Christ. When the church fails to speak

the Word of God into culture, culture cannot be redeemed for the Lord's purposes.

The Unchanging Principles of the Bible

We know God and therefore should wed our beliefs to the unchanging principles of the Bible and not to fickle cultural practices. Because we know God and we celebrate the gift of Christian liberty, the cultural choices of others (even if we do not like them) that do not violate God's moral will should be a source of joy for us, not a source of agitation.

With a developed Christian worldview, Christians should be able to exercise our spiritual discernment on all matters of faith and practice and do this in a manner that expresses love for our neighbors while encouraging fellowship with other believers. The great reformer Martin Luther said it best: "In essentials, unity, in nonessentials, liberty, in all things, charity."

Insofar as we submit our likes and dislikes, including our fears and excitement about social changes, to the Spirit of God, he will develop a right spirit within us. He will be our Counselor and Comforter in the face of social change and the temptation to enter into culture wars.

CULTURAL PUZZLES

Modernity is about the new, but like all things once new, there comes a time when it becomes old and may someday pass into history. Modernity is just a label. It's a name we've given to a period of history and the values and social changes that seem to characterize it. Modernity has given us incredible technological, transportation, and communication advances. We've enjoyed a period that has added immeasurably to our lives in terms of creature comforts, even as the primary assumptions of Modernity's underlying philosophy have eroded some of the foundations of our existence.

Our modern neighbors have premised their drive for earthly utopia on the assumption that objective truth can be known through human reason and science and that inevitable, evolutionary progress will result. Our modern neighbors anticipated a secular, not supernatural, utopia because they thought religion, though sometimes helpful as a kind of social glue, was nevertheless expendable. Progress and prosperity, created by vast bureaucracies in a capitalistic economy based on human ingenuity, were supposedly all we needed for the good life.

But Modernity is getting old, and its aspiration for a secular utopia on earth remains unfulfilled, in part because many of the modern mentality's assumptions about life have proved false. World wars, economic recessions, disease, crime, violence, racism, and religious and ethnic conflict are only a few of the chronic human ills modern philosophy and technology have not been able to fix.

Everyone's Own Truth

Now a fading Modernity is overlapping with an emerging Postmodernity. The new postmodern mentality still considers human beings autonomous but rejects the idea of knowable objective truth and questions the very idea of progress. This postmodern mentality says that if truth exists at all, it exists only as an expression of a given person's interpretation of the world. Truth is intuitive, subjective, or culturally conditioned. Truth is whatever you want it to be. Doubting whether any grand paradigm capable of explaining all of life is even possible, our postmodern neighbors reduce religion, philosophy, education, law, ethics, and politics to the mundane, to the most minute and arcane details that provide little evidence of connectedness or principled significance.

This reductionism or minimalizing applies to God as well. The modern mentality has gradually assumed God's irrelevance, then finally has denied his existence. As we have seen, the postmodern mentality is less aggressively secular than the modern mentality, but the postmodern mentality worships innumerable gods, not the one true God. Ironically, the postmodern mentality offers us many values, religions, and gods to choose from at a time when not much confidence in values, religion, or God remains. Of course we know that nature abhors a vacuum; so if Christ is not at the center of culture, an idol will be.[5] Consequently, in the postmodern culture emerging around us, many people worship idols of their own choosing.

Moral Relativism

Without God, without universal truth, our postmodern neighbors gradually become centerless, floating chaotically in a universe with no Son creating a meaningful orbit. Since no common standards hold culture together, diversity is celebrated at the expense of unity. The result is a continuing breakdown of any kind of public moral consensus on issues fundamental to secure, healthy, and productive lives. While traditional values still influence American culture, it is no longer possible to say that these values—least of all specifically Christian values—dominate America's understanding of morality. For the postmodern mentality, the seemingly apathetic but philosophically potent teenage response—"Whatever"—is all there is.

This "whatever" approach to life affects Christians too. One of the principal challenges in any Christian college or university today is simply getting students (most of whom claim to be Christians) to recognize that standards, principles, or absolute values of any kind actually exist and should be allowed to govern our lives. This "whatever" approach of the postmodern mentality is evident in students' attitudes toward integrity of their own word, punctuality, campus traffic and parking policies, a work ethic, academic work and grades, and personal sexual morality. Even many Christians, it seems, often want to live life without parameters, doing what is right in their own eyes in any given situation.

Depending on whom you associate with on a daily basis, it may be difficult for you to understand just how "absolutely" our postmodern neighbors hold to their moral relativism. For most of them, moral relativism is probably not expressed as a form of outright anarchy—running naked through the streets or staging all-night debaucheries. Our neighbors' expression of moral relativism is generally a bit more subtle, seen in, for example, their attitudes toward marital fidelity, divorce, abortion, gambling, or language, to name a few. And as would be expected, these attitudes affect how they live their lives in rather practical ways.

However moral relativism is expressed, its accumulated impact on individuals and on culture is still ultimately devastating. Moral relativism produces social degradation, then debilitation, then disintegration, and ultimately destruction. Individuals who reject God and embrace "morality-as-choice" follow a similar path: uncertainty, then anxiety, then loss of hope, then despair, then alienation, then cynicism, then rage. In the case of either society or individuals, it is not just rhetoric to make the observation that moral relativism, the defining characteristic of postmodern culture, is a centrifugal force carrying within it a destructive capacity reminiscent of Sodom and Gomorrah.

TRUTH OR CONSEQUENCES

All human beings live on a spiritual death row. How do we know this? Because the Bible says, "For the wages of sin is death, but the gift of God is eternal life in Christ Jesus our Lord" (Rom. 6:23). Because of humanity's fall into sin described in Genesis 3, each human being is either a sinner saved by grace or a sinner in need of grace. God, through Jesus Christ, is the only one who can pardon us from our spiritual death penalty. That's the truth of the human condition. That's reality.

If something is not true, it's not real. It doesn't fit reality, so it can't be true. Even as our postmodern neighbors have rejected truth, they've hungered for what's real. Whether they're living materially and emotionally blessed lives or lives of quiet desperation, they want authenticity. They may not know it, but that's their cry for help, and it's the Christian's opportunity.

People possess a divinely given sense of person, presence, and purpose. All human beings distinguish themselves from others; all of us know that we are here now, alive in this world; and all of us know or want to know why we are here. People must look somewhere to connect and fulfill these needs, and for the most part, people look for a secular redeemer.[6] They do not realize that "the god of this age has blinded the minds of unbelievers, so that they cannot see the light of the gospel of the glory of Christ" (2 Cor. 4:4).

We find our Christian opportunity and responsibility, our stewardship, in this PoMo sense of centerlessness. In this place we can and should ask our postmodern neighbors to consider what guides us. Is it Providence, Manifest Destiny, some kind of spirit or fate, a dialectic?[7] Or is it the redemptive character of history? The advantage of the Christian worldview is that it fits with the real world and conveys truth in every way. All other worldviews ultimately fail to explain reality or meet people's need for a faithful witness to their divinely appointed sense of person, presence, and purpose.

All men and women have faith, but for that faith to be effective it must be placed in the sovereign God, both personal and infinite, who works in history, reveals himself in his Son and his Word, and is truly God. Unlike the faiths of postmodern culture, the "Christian faith is not a leap in the dark, nor faith in faith, nor faith in blind authority. It is far from radical uncertainty. It is the firm conviction that the self-disclosure of God in Jesus Christ is the ultimate truth of what is. It is a reasonable decision after rational reflection."[8]

The darker in its outlook postmodern culture becomes, the more brightly the light of the gospel will shine, and it should shine most vividly through Christians who go into the world to evangelize the lost and transform culture for Christ.

Christians can fulfill their calling in the Cultural Mandate and the Great Commission by evidencing in their lives that they believe history is going somewhere, that it has a goal—the kingdom of God. As we are able to demonstrate that the function of social history is redemptive, that the definition of history lies outside of history in God, and that we are able to know this God who is truth, we will share our light with our postmodern neighbors.

Change is a double-edged sword. Change may be inevitable but not certain patterns of change. Of Postmodernity we may safely say, "This too shall pass," because even postmodern culture is changing to something else. Though the assumption that truth does not exist is spiritually and culturally deadly and is something Christians must take seriously, it is not unassailable. Moral relativism is not invincible because it is not true. Christians must not forget that postmodern culture is built on a lie, what the Scripture calls a "powerful delusion" (2 Thess. 2:11). People "deliberately forget that long ago by God's word the heavens existed and the earth was formed" (2 Peter 3:5). Because they are free to do so, people may deny creation, they may deny their humanness, they may deny God himself, but in the end they are "slaves of depravity—for a man is a slave to whatever has mastered him" (2:19).

The intellectual gymnastics of this world are simply hollow philosophy to God:

> For the message of the cross is foolishness to those who are perishing, but to us who are being saved it is the power of God. For it is

written: "I will destroy the wisdom of the wise; the intelligence of the intelligent will I frustrate." Where is the wise man? Where is the scholar? Where is the philosopher of this age? Has not God made foolish the wisdom of the world?

1 Corinthians 1:18–20

In case you missed it, the point is that Christians can change change. Indeed, we are compelled to change things to make them what God desires for his kingdom. "Scripture destroys the myths of the age, any age."[9] That is the advantage of a biblical Christian worldview. This is the command of the Cultural Mandate and the Great Commission.

Our postmodern neighbors need spiritual *regeneration,* and our culture needs biblical, spiritual *reformation.* For this to take place, we must begin with ourselves. We need *revival,* a matter for the Christian church, "for it is time for judgment to begin with the family of God" (1 Peter 4:17). Revival happens when God's people focus on obedience to God's Word. We know that revival, as well as regeneration and reformation, is possible when orthodoxy is rediscovered and implemented, as the historical examples of the Old Testament Israelites and of Martin Luther's Reformation attest.

Regeneration occurs in the nonbeliever's confession of faith in Christ (Rom. 10:9–10). "At the end of the day, being a Christian isn't about being ancient, medieval, modern, or postmodern. It's about following Jesus, becoming more like him, participating in the kingdom he announced and invited us into, serving him."[10] Regeneration must precede reformation if reform is to be lasting.[11]

> The history of Christianity is filled with glorious demonstrations of the truth and power of the Gospel. Through the centuries, when Christians have lived out their faith by putting both the cultural commission and the great commission to work, they have renewed, restored, and on occasions, even built new cultures. They have literally turned the world upside down. [12]

Spiritual reformation is inevitably followed by social change.[13]

UNTIL I COME BACK

God never said to abandon and run; he said, "Work until I come back" (see Luke 19:13).

> Paul urges Timothy to recognize his battle-torn circumstances and not to relax his vigilance (1 Tim. 1:18; 4:16; 6:12, etc.). The moment he ceases to believe that he's at war he'll get caught up with secondary issues and fail to satisfy his commander (2 Tim. 2:4). Part of the trouble with many churches today is that they no longer see themselves in a battle situation. They demonstrate no alertness to what is happening to them and, accepting everything that comes their way, do not have any desire to make an impact on the world around them.[14]

We cannot afford this kind of spiritual sleepiness any longer. We must be "men and women of Issachar," alert, informed, and in God's service.

I want to summarize what we've learned in nine principles for practice. These principles will allow us to be "men and women of Issachar" in a rapidly changing world:

1. Affirm biblical Christianity, nothing more, nothing less, and personal, saving faith in Jesus Christ, who is "the way, the truth, and the life."
2. Develop a biblically Christian worldview, which yields spiritual discernment capable of distinguishing truth from error as well as what is best in culture.
3. Learn to anticipate change as much as order, for both are part of God's sovereign design for this world.
4. Live biblically with the "in the world/not of the world tension," by applying Christian liberty and recognizing that biblical Christianity is not about rules but about a relationship with Christ.
5. Work to evangelize the lost, edify the saints, and transform the culture for the cause of Christ, thus obeying God's Cultural Mandate and Great Commission.
6. Enjoy Postmodernity, developing its potential, ministering to its problems, creating culture.

7. Combat postmodernism, particularly its moral relativism, while creatively applying biblical truths to the individual and cultural questions and needs which have been created by the postmodern mentality.

8. Model community in the Christian church based on a biblical understanding of unity and diversity.

9. Go into the world, speaking the truth in love to PoMo people, first showing them love so that they can hear the truth.

God did not leave Christians without resources. He gave us in his Word everything we need for a life of godliness and a life characterized by fulfillment of his purposes for the church and culture in his world. He gave us the Holy Spirit to develop our knowledge of his Word and enable us to both confront a culture tainted by sin and create a culture to the glory of God. This includes any period of history and any kind of social change. No change surprises God. No change should frighten those of us who are his children.

The Christian faith has stood the test of time, though Christians have sometimes buckled under the stress of social change. But always remember, we draw our strength from Christ, who is "the same yesterday, today, and forever."

NOTES

Introduction *Christian Themes in Changing Times*

1. Mark A. Noll, "Christian World Views and Some Lessons of History," in Arthur F. Holmes, ed., *The Making of a Christian Mind: A Christian Worldview and the Academic Enterprise* (Downers Grove, Ill.: InterVarsity Press, 1985), 29. See also Mark A. Noll, *The Scandal of the Evangelical Mind* (Downers Grove, Ill.: InterVarsity Press, 1994).

2. Harry Blamires, *The Christian Mind: How Should a Christian Mind Think?* (Ann Arbor, Mich.: Servant, 1963), 3.

3. Quoted in Os Guinness, *Fit Bodies, Fat Minds: Why Evangelicals Don't Think and What to Do about It* (Grand Rapids: Baker, 1994), 12.

4. I owe Dr. Victoria Swenson, Cornerstone University, for this pungent quote.

5. Holmes, ed., *Making of a Christian Mind,* 11.

6. The Hebrew word for *neighbor* in Leviticus 19:18 is *rea*. In the New Testament the Greek word for neighbor, *perioikos,* meaning "housed around," is used only once. The Greek word meaning "adjoining one's ground" is *geiton* and is used four times. The Greek word *plesion* means "close by, fellow, Christian, associate, friend, countryman, man, companion, stranger."

7. H. Henry Meeter, *The Basic Ideas of Calvinism* (Grand Rapids: Baker, 1956), 175.

8. John Wecks, *Free to Disagree: Moving Beyond the Arguments over Christian Liberty* (Grand Rapids: Kregel, 1996), 136–37.

9. Richard S. Taylor says, "As nature is the gift of God, culture is the work of man" (*A Return to Christian Culture* [Minneapolis: Dimension Books, 1973], 12).

10. Francis A. Schaeffer, *How Shall We Then Live? The Rise and Decline of Western Thought and Culture* (Old Tappan, N.J.: Revell, 1976).

Chapter 1 *Changing Times*

1. Henry R. Van Til, *The Calvinistic Concept of Culture* (Grand Rapids: Baker, 1959), 7, 29–30.

2. T. S. Eliot, *Notes toward a Definition of Culture* (New York: Harcourt and Brace, 1949), 30.

3. See Taylor, *Return to Christian Culture,* 12; and Van Til, *Calvinistic Concept of Culture,* 21, 42.

4. Fyodor Dostoyevsky, *The Brothers Karamazov* (Harmandsworth, Middlesex, England: Penguin, 1958), 733.

5. Cited in Os Guinness, *The Dust of Death: The Sixties Counterculture and How It Changed America Forever* (Wheaton, Ill.: Crossway, 1994), 322.

6. Marvin K. Mayers, *Christianity Confronts Culture: A Strategy for Cross-Cultural Evangelism* (Grand Rapids: Zondervan, 1974), 15.

7. For an interesting look at language, see Terry M. Crist, *Learning the Language of Babylon: Changing the World by Engaging the Culture* (Grand Rapids: Chosen, 2001).

8. Ibid., 35.

9. Charles Colson and Nancy Pearcey, *The Christian in Today's Culture* (Wheaton, Ill.: Tyndale, 2001), x.

10. H. R. Rookmaaker, *Modern Art and the Death of a Culture* (London: Inter-Varsity Press, 1970), 198.

Chapter 2 *Developing a Christian Worldview*

1. Guinness, *The Dust of Death,* 25.

2. Francis A. Schaeffer, *The Church at the End of the Twentieth Century* (Downers Grove, Ill.: InterVarsity Press, 1970), 14.

3. Abraham Kuyper, *Christianity as a Life System: The Witness of a Worldview* (Memphis: Christian Studies Center, 1980).

4. James W. Sire, *The Universe Next Door: A Basic Worldview Catalog* (Downers Grove, Ill.: InterVarsity Press, 1988), 17.

5. Arthur F. Holmes, *Contours of a Worldview* (Grand Rapids: Eerdmans, 1983), 34.

6. J. Richard Middleton and Brian J. Walsh, *Truth Is Stranger Than It Used to Be: Biblical Faith in a Postmodern Age* (Grand Rapids: Eerdmans, 1995), 11.

7. See Herman Dooyeweerd, *In the Twilight of Western Thought: Studies in the Pretended Autonomy of Philosophical Thought* (Lewiston, N.Y.: E. Mellen, 1999); and Alan Storkey, *A Christian Social Perspective* (Downers Grove, Ill.: InterVarsity Press, 1979), 27.

8. This is epistemology, the study of how one knows or how one determines knowledge.

9. Dooyeweerd, *In the Twilight of Western Thought,* xv.

10. Ibid., ix.

11. Van Til, *Calvinistic Concept of Culture,* 200.

12. See a similar discussion in Holmes, *Contours of a Worldview.*

13. Cited in Schaeffer, *Church at the End of the Twentieth Century,* 10.

14. Guinness, *The Dust of Death,* 346–54.

15. Francis A. Schaeffer, *The God Who Is There* (Downers Grove, Ill.: Inter-Varsity Press, 1968); and *He Is There and He Is Not Silent* (Wheaton, Ill.: Tyndale, 1972).

16. Charles Colson and Nancy Pearcey, *How Now Shall We Live?* (Wheaton, Ill.: Tyndale, 1999), 33–34.

17. Bruce A. Little, "Christian Education, Worldviews, and Postmodernity's Challenge," *Journal of the Evangelical Theological Society* 40, no. 3 (September 1997): 440.

18. Schaeffer, *He Is There and He Is Not Silent,* 79; and Schaeffer, *Church at the End of the Twentieth Century,* 53.

19. Arthur F. Holmes, *All Truth Is God's Truth* (Grand Rapids: Eerdmans, 1977), 8; and Arthur F. Holmes, *The Idea of a Christian College,* rev. ed. (Grand Rapids: Eerdmans, 1987), 58.

20. Holmes, ed., *Making of a Christian Mind,* 12.

21. Colson and Pearcey, *How Now Shall We Live?,* 384–91; Van Til, *Calvinistic Concept of Culture,* 217–20; Holmes, *Contours of a Worldview,* 214–22; and Holmes, *All Truth Is God's Truth,* 16–27.

22. For an excellent and relatively brief examination of the concept of Christian calling, see Henlee H. Barnette, *Christian Calling and Vocation* (Grand Rapids: Baker, 1965).

23. S. D. Gaede, *Where Gods May Dwell: Understanding the Human Condition* (Grand Rapids: Zondervan, 1985), 98, 109; and Taylor, *Return to Christian Culture,* 50.

Chapter 3 *Christian Views of Social Change*

1. Colson and Pearcey, *How Now Shall We Live?,* 54.

2. For a discussion of ancient cyclical views of history, see David W. Bebbington, *Patterns in History: A Christian View* (Downers Grove, Ill.: InterVarsity Press, 1979), 21–42.

3. Guinness, *The Dust of Death,* 333.

4. J. I. Packer, *Knowing God* (Downers Grove, Ill.: InterVarsity Press, 1993).

5. See Bebbington, *Patterns in History,* 34; and Robert A. Nisbet, *Social Change and History: Aspects of the Western Theology of Development* (New York: Oxford University Press, 1969), 64, 82–83, 211–17.

6. Schaeffer, *He Is There and He Is Not Silent,* 62–63.

7. See Robert A. Nisbet, *History of the Idea of Progress* (New York: Basic Books, 1980); and David Lyon, *Future Society: Life after 1984—Threat or Promise?* (Belleville, Mich.: Lion, 1984), 19.

8. Garry Friesen, *Decision Making and the Will of God* (Portland: Multnomah, 1980), 201–8.

9. Ibid., 205.

10. Derek Tidball, *The Social Context of the New Testament: A Sociological Analysis* (Grand Rapids: Zondervan, 1984), 138–39.

11. Friesen, *Decision Making and the Will of God,* 232; illustration used by permission.

12. From E. H. Harbison, *Christianity and History* (Princeton, N.J.: Princeton University Press, 1964), 288; and cited in Bebbington, *Patterns in History,* 67.

13. I owe most of this paragraph to Albert M. Wolters, *Creation Regained: Biblical Basis for a Reformational Worldview* (Grand Rapids: Eerdmans, 1985), 11, 57–58, 60, 64.

Chapter 4   *Spiritual Discernment*

1. This is Cornerstone University's mission statement.

2. Kenneth Scott Latourette, *A History of Christianity* (New York: Harper and Row, 1953), 22.

3. Shaunti Feldhahn, *The Veritas Conflict* (Sisters, Ore.: Multnomah, 2001), 124–25.

4. Luke Timothy Johnson, *Scripture and Discernment: Decision-Making in the Church* (Nashville: Abingdon, 1996), 109–10.

5. See Lausanne Theology and Education Group, *The Willowbank Report,* prepared at the Consultation on Gospel and Culture (Somerset Bridge, Bermuda, January 13, 1978), 454–56.

6. H. R. Inge, quoted in Herbert Schlossberg, *Idols of Destruction: Christian Faith and Its Confrontation with American Society* (Washington, D.C.: Regnery Gateway, 1990), 9.

7. Van Til, *Calvinistic Concept of Culture,* 35.

8. Francis A. Schaeffer, *A Christian Manifesto* (Westchester, Ill.: Crossway, 1981), 20; and Schaeffer, *He Is There and He Is Not Silent,* 47.

Chapter 5   *Rediscovering Christian Liberty*

1. Cited in Guinness, *The Dust of Death,* 320.

2. See George Downame, *The Christian's Freedom* (1835; reprint, Pittsburgh: Soli Deo Gloria Publishers, 1994).

3. Donald R. Wilson, "Cultural Relativism," *Baker's Dictionary of Christian Ethics,* (Grand Rapids: Baker Books, 1973), 157.

4. Elisabeth Elliot, *The Liberty of Obedience: Some Thoughts on Christian Conduct and Service* (Waco: Word, 1968), 22.

5. Carl G. Kromminga, "Christian Love and Offending the 'Weak': A Review Article." *Calvin Theological Journal* 28 (1993): 158.

6. Van Til, *Calvinistic Concept of Culture,* 27.

7. See Rex M. Rogers, *Seducing America: Is Gambling a Good Bet?* (Grand Rapids: Baker, 1997), 60–61.

8. In listing these preferences, I am not saying that I necessarily endorse them all or that I have participated personally in them all, only that these things are not specifically addressed in Scripture and therefore have been the subject of much Christian debate.

9. James D. G. Dunn, *Christian Liberty: A New Testament Perspective* (Grand Rapids: Eerdmans, 1993), 54.

10. Ibid., 95.

11. Wecks, *Free to Disagree,* 39.

12. John Calvin, *Institutes of the Christian Religion,* vol. 2, trans. John Allen (Philadelphia: Presbyterian Board of Christian Education, 1932), 72.

13. Kromminga, "Christian Love and Offending the 'Weak,'" 161.

14. Ibid., 160.

15. Ibid., 156.

16. Ibid., 160.

17. Calvin, *Institutes,* 70.

18. Wecks, *Free to Disagree,* 82.

19. Kromminga, "Christian Love and Offending the 'Weak,'" 157, 160.

20. Ibid., 160.

21. Calvin, *Institutes,* 72.

22. Ibid.

23. Kromminga, "Christian Love and Offending the 'Weak,'" 163.

24. Martin Luther, "On the Freedom of a Christian Man," cited in Friesen, *Decision Making and the Will of God,* 401.

25. Calvin, *Institutes,* 63.

26. Schaeffer, *Church at the End of the Twentieth Century,* 67; emphasis added.

Chapter 6 *Modernity to Postmodernity*

1. For an original look at *Star Trek*'s reflection of contemporary culture, see the insightful work of Stanley J. Grenz, "Star Trek and the Next Generation: Postmodernism and the Future of Evangelical Theology," in David S. Dockery, ed., *The Challenge of Postmodernism: An Evangelical Engagement* (Wheaton, Ill.: Victor, 1995), 89–103; see also www.startrek.com/library/bios.asp for cast and crew biographies and www.startrek.com/information/timeline.asp for more information on the *Star Trek* series.

2. Bebbington, *Patterns in History,* 171–72.

3. Earl E. Cairns, *God and Man in Time: A Christian Approach to Historiography* (Grand Rapids: Baker, 1979), 79, 109–10.

4. Millard J. Erickson, *Postmodernizing the Faith: Evangelical Responses to the Challenge of Postmodernism* (Grand Rapids: Baker, 1998), 15–16.

5. Paul Meadows, *The Many Faces of Change: Explorations in the Theory of Social Change* (Cambridge, Mass.: Schenkman, 1971), 21.

6. Stanley J. Grenz, *A Primer on Postmodernism* (Grand Rapids: Eerdmans, 1996), 4.

7. David Lyon, *Postmodernity,* 2d ed. (Minneapolis: University of Minnesota Press, 1999), 7.

8. Peter Jones, *Spirit Wars: Pagan Revival in Christian America* (Mukilteo, Wash.: WinePress, 1997), 20.

9. Bebbington, *Patterns in History,* 68.

10. Middleton and Walsh, *Truth Is Stranger Than It Used to Be,* 15, 18–20.

11. Anthony D. Smith, *The Concept of Social Change* (London: Routledge and Kegan Paul, 1973), 147.

12. David Lyon, "Rethinking Secularization: Retrospect and Prospect," *Review of Religious Research* 26, no. 3 (March 1985): 228–43.

13. Robert Wuthnow, *The Struggle for America's Soul: Evangelicals, Liberals, and Secularism* (Grand Rapids: Eerdmans, 1989), 116–25; and Tom Sine, *Wild Hope: Crises Facing the Human Community on the Threshold of the 21st Century* (Dallas: Word, 1991), 188–89.

14. See Peter L. Berger, *The Heretical Imperative: Contemporary Possibilities of Religious Affirmation* (Garden City, N.Y.: Doubleday, 1979); and a Christian critique of Berger's argument in Leslie Newbigin, *Foolishness to the Greeks: The Gospel and Western Culture* (Grand Rapids: Eerdmans, 1986).

15. J. A. Walter, *Sacred Cows: Exploring Contemporary Idolatry* (Grand Rapids: Zondervan, 1979), 182.

16. See Jones, *Spirit Wars*; and Walter, *Sacred Cows*.

17. See David S. Dockery and David P. Gushee, eds., *The Future of Christian Higher Education* (Nashville: Broadman and Holman, 1999); George M. Marsden and Bradley J. Longfield, eds., *The Secularization of the Academy* (New York: Oxford University Press, 1992); George M. Marsden, *The Soul of the American University* (New York: Oxford University Press, 1994).

18. Grenz, *Primer on Postmodernism,* 17; and Guinness, *Fit Bodies, Fat Minds,* 104.

19. Grenz, *Primer on Postmodernism,* 12.

20. Paul Lakeland, *Postmodernity: Christian Identity in a Fragmented Age* (Minneapolis: Fortress, 1997), 59.

21. Grenz, *Primer on Postmodernism,* 7.

22. Ibid., 14; emphasis added.

23. Ibid., 15.

24. Ibid., 7, 15, 18, 29.

25. Ibid., 44.

26. Lakeland, *Postmodernity,* 7.

27. Lyon, *Postmodernity,* 9, 11–12, 14.

28. Guinness, *Fit Bodies, Fat Minds,* 106.

29. Lyon, *Postmodernity,* 9.

Chapter 7 *The Postmodern Culture*

1. Gene Edward Veith Jr., *Postmodern Times: A Christian Guide to Contemporary Thought and Culture* (Wheaton, Ill.: Crossway, 1994), 49.

2. Os Guinness, *The American Hour: A Time of Reckoning and the Once and Future Role of Faith* (New York: Free Press, 1993), 28.

3. Veith, *Postmodern Times,* xii.

4. Ibid., 20.

5. Erickson, *Postmodernizing the Faith,* 17.

6. Schaeffer, *He Is There and He Is Not Silent,* 23.

7. Erickson, *Postmodernizing the Faith,* 11; and Walter, *Sacred Cows,* 182.

8. Grenz, *Primer on Postmodernism,* 20.

9. Guinness, *Fit Bodies, Fat Minds,* 49–54.

10. Alexander Hamilton, James Madison, and John Jay, *The Federalist Papers,* prepared by Clinton Rossiter (New York: The New American Library, 1961), Federalist Paper #10, 77–84.

11. See Peter L. Berger, *The Sacred Canopy: Elements of a Sociological Theory of Religion* (Garden City, N.Y.: Doubleday, 1967); and Richard John Neuhaus, *The Naked Public Square: Religion and Democracy in America* (Grand Rapids: Eerdmans, 1984).

12. See James Davison Hunter, *Culture Wars: The Struggle to Define America* (New York: Basic Books, 1991).

13. Douglas Groothuis, "The Smorgasbord Mentality," *Eternity* (May 1985): 33.

14. Guinness, *The American Hour,* 65.

15. William D. Watkins, *The New Absolutes: How They Are Being Imposed on Us and How They Are Eroding Our Moral Landscape* (Minneapolis: Bethany, 1996), 23.

16. Lakeland, *Postmodernity,* 27.

17. See Watkins, *New Absolutes;* Jones, *Spirit Wars;* and Alan Wolfe, *Moral Freedom: The Impossible Idea That Defines the Way We Live Now* (New York: Norton, 2001).

18. Guinness, *The American Hour,* 31.

19. Groothuis, "The Smorgasbord Mentality," 33.

20. Wolfe, *Moral Freedom,* 195, 199, 200, 203, 228; emphasis added.

21. Grenz, *Primer on Postmodernism,* 31.

22. Ibid., 37–38.

23. Ibid., 19.

24. Middleton and Walsh, *Truth Is Stranger Than It Used to Be,* 54.

25. Grenz, *Primer on Postmodernism,* 37.

26. Ibid., 15.

27. Guinness, *Fit Bodies, Fat Minds,* 105.

28. Charles Colson, "More Doctrine, Not Less," at http://www.christianity-today.com/ct/2002/005/31.96.html.

29. Brian D. McLaren, *The Church on the Other Side: Doing Ministry in the Post-modern Matrix* (Grand Rapids: Zondervan, 2000), 70.

30. Guinness, *Fit Bodies, Fat Minds,* 51; and Colson and Pearcey, *How Now Shall We Live?,* 21.

31. Veith, *Postmodern Times,* 51, 57, 59; Guinness, *The American Hour,* 70; and Rex M. Rogers, "On Becoming a University," Grand Rapids: Cornerstone University, 2002.

32. Rex M. Rogers, "Moral Relativism, Christian Enemy," *Voice* (September/October 1994): 19.

33. Psychologist Arthur Kroker, quoted in Veith, *Postmodern Times,* 82–83.

Chapter 8 *Christian Culture Wars*

1. George Barna, cited in Dockery and Gushee, eds., *Future of Christian Higher Education*, 8.

2. These last few sentences are a paraphrase from Van Til, *Calvinistic Concept of Culture*, 35.

3. Kenneth Scott Latourette, *A History of Christianity* (New York: Harper and Row, 1953).

4. See Rogers, *Seducing America*.

5. Wecks, *Free to Disagree*, 14–15.

6. Van Til, *Calvinistic Concept of Culture*, 220.

7. Taylor, *Return to Christian Culture*, 81.

8. See for example a related discussion in Elliot, *The Liberty of Obedience.*

9. Stephen Scott, *Why Do They Dress That Way?* (Intercourse, Pa.: Good Books, 1986).

10. Tidball, *Social Context of the New Testament*, 135.

11. Schaeffer, *Church at the End of the Twentieth Century*, 81.

12. Dunn, *Christian Liberty*, 90.

13. Schaeffer, *Church at the End of the Twentieth Century*, 76–77.

14. Cited in Crist, *Learning the Language of Babylon*, 9.

15. Elliot, *Liberty of Obedience*, 58.

Chapter 9 *Christians in a PoMo Culture*

1. Walter, *Sacred Cows*, 22.

2. McLaren, *Church on the Other Side*, 177.

3. Ibid., 179.

4. Colson and Pearcey, *How Now Shall We Live?*, 17; emphasis added.

5. Hunter, *Culture Wars*, 42.

6. McLaren, *Church on the Other Side*, 70.

7. Crist, *Learning the Language of Babylon*, 55.

8. Darrell L. Guder, ed., *Missional Church: A Vision for the Sending of the Church in North America* (Grand Rapids: Eerdmans, 1998), 114; emphasis added.

9. See Rex M. Rogers, "Toward a Public Morality" (Cornerstone University, 1995, pamphlet).

10. Cited in Guinness, *Fit Bodies, Fat Minds*, 66.

11. Bebbington, *Patterns in History*, 50–51.

12. Lyon, *Future Society*, 126.

13. Hamilton, Madison, and Jay, *The Federalist Papers*, Federalist Paper #2, 39.

Chapter 10 *Making the Most of Every Opportunity*

1. I owe this understanding to Dr. Michael Wittmer, "Fundamentals of a Christian Worldview" (audiotaped lectures at Grand Rapids Baptist Seminary of Cornerstone University, fall 2001).

2. Lyon, "Rethinking Secularization," 239.

3. David O. Moberg, *The Church as a Social Institution*, 2d ed. (Grand Rapids: Baker, 1984), 519; and Tidball, *Social Context of the New Testament*, 123–36.

4. Walter, *Sacred Cows*, 167.

5. Newbigin, *Foolishness to the Greeks*, 115.

6. Meadows, *The Many Faces of Change*, 41; and Nisbet, *History of the Idea of Progress*, 351.

7. Nisbet, *Social Change and History*, 77.

8. Guinness, *Dust of Death*, 355.

9. Schlossberg, *Idols of Destruction*, 300.

10. McLaren, *Church on the Other Side*, 201.

11. Cairns, *God and Man in Time*, 18.

12. Colson and Pearcey, *How Now Shall We Live?*, 298.

13. Ibid., 302.

14. Tidball, *Social Context of the New Testament*, 135.

SELECTED BIBLIOGRAPHY

Applebaum, Richard. *Theories of Social Change.* Chicago: Markham, 1970.

Arndt, William. "Galatians—A Declaration of Christian Liberty." *Concordia Theological Monthly* 28, no. 9 (September 1956): 673–92.

Barnette, Henlee H. *Christian Calling and Vocation.* Grand Rapids: Baker, 1965.

Bebbington, David W. *Patterns in History: A Christian View.* Downers Grove, Ill.: InterVarsity Press, 1979.

Bellah, Robert N., Richard Madsen, William M. Sullivan, Ann Swidler, and Steven M. Tipton. *Habits of the Heart: Individualism and Commitment in American Life.* Berkeley: University of California Press, 1985.

Berger, Peter L. *The Sacred Canopy: Elements of a Sociological Theory of Religion.* Garden City, N.Y.: Doubleday, 1967.

Berger, Peter L., Brigitte Berger, and Hansfried Kellner. *The Homeless Mind: Modernization and Consciousness.* New York: Random House, 1974.

Billingsley, K. L. *The Seductive Image: A Christian Critique of the World of Film.* Westchester, Ill.: Crossway, 1989.

Blamires, Harry. *The Christian Mind: How Should a Christian Mind Think?* Ann Arbor, Mich.: Servant, 1963.

Cairns, Earl E. *God and Man in Time: A Christian Approach to Historiography.* Grand Rapids: Baker, 1979.

Calvin, John, "On Christian Liberty." In *Institutes of the Christian Religion.* Vol. 2. Translated by John Allen. 6th American rev. ed. Philadelphia: Presbyterian Board of Christian Education, 1932.

Carter, Stephen L. *The Culture of Disbelief: How American Law and Politics Trivialize Religious Devotion.* New York: Doubleday, 1993.

Clark, Gordon H. *A Christian Philosophy of Education.* 1946. Reprint, Jefferson, Md.: The Trinity Foundation, 1988.

Colson, Charles, and Nancy Pearcey. *The Christian in Today's Culture.* Wheaton, Ill.: Tyndale, 2001.

———. *How Now Shall We Live?* Wheaton, Ill.: Tyndale, 1999.

Cox, Harvey. *Religion in the Secular City: Toward a Postmodern Theology.* New York: Simon and Schuster, 1984.

Crist, Terry M. *Learning the Language of Babylon: Changing the World by Engaging the Culture.* Grand Rapids: Chosen, 2001.

Dockery, David S., ed. *The Challenge of Postmodernism: An Evangelical Engagement.* 2d ed. Grand Rapids: Baker, 2001.

Dooyeweerd, Hermann. *In the Twilight of Western Thought: Studies in the Pretended Autonomy of Philosophical Thought.* Lewiston, N.Y.: E. Mellen, 1999.

Downame, George. *The Christian's Freedom.* 1835. Reprint, Pittsburgh: Soli Deo Gloria, 1994.

Dunn, James D. G. *Christian Liberty: A New Testament Perspective.* Grand Rapids: Eerdmans, 1993.

Eliot, T. S. *Notes toward a Definition of Culture.* New York: Harcourt and Brace, 1949.

Elliot, Elisabeth. *The Liberty of Obedience: Some Thoughts on Christian Conduct and Service.* Waco: Word, 1968.

Ellul, Jacques. *The Technological Society.* New York: Vintage, 1964.

———. *The Technological System.* New York: Continuum, 1980.

Erickson, Millard J. *Postmodernizing the Faith: Evangelical Responses to the Challenge of Postmodernism.* Grand Rapids: Baker, 1998.

Feldhahn, Shaunti. *The Veritas Conflict.* Sisters, Ore.: Multnomah, 2001.

Freisen, Garry. *Decision Making and the Will of God.* Portland: Multnomah, 1980.

Gaede, S. D. *Where Gods May Dwell: Understanding the Human Condition.* Grand Rapids: Zondervan, 1985.

Good, Merle and Phyllis. *20 Most Asked Questions about the Amish
and Mennonites.* Lancaster, Pa.: Good Books, 1979.

Grenz, Stanley J. *A Primer on Postmodernism.* Grand Rapids: Eerdmans, 1996.

Guder, Darrell L., ed. *Missional Church: A Vision for the Sending of the
Church in North America.* Grand Rapids: Eerdmans, 1998.

Guinness, Os. *The American Hour: A Time of Reckoning and the Once
and Future Role of Faith.* New York: Free Press, 1993.

————. *The Dust of Death: The Sixties Counterculture and How It
Changed America Forever.* Wheaton, Ill.: Crossway, 1994.

————. *Fit Bodies, Fat Minds: Why Evangelicals Don't Think and What
to Do about It.* Grand Rapids: Baker, 1994.

Henry, Carl F. H. *The Christian Mindset in a Secular Society: Promoting
Evangelical Renewal and National Righteousness.* Portland, Ore.: Multnomah, 1978.

Heslam, Peter S. *Creating a Christian Worldview: Abraham Kuyper's Lectures on Calvinism.* Grand Rapids: Eerdmans, 1998.

Hoffecker, W. Andrew, and Gary Scott Smith, eds. *Building a Christian Worldview.* Vol. 1. *God, Man, and Knowledge.* Phillipsburg, N.J.:
Presbyterian and Reformed, 1986.

Holmes, Arthur F. *All Truth Is God's Truth.* Grand Rapids: Eerdmans,
1977.

————. *Contours of a Worldview.* Grand Rapids: Eerdmans, 1983.

————. *The Idea of a Christian College.* Rev. ed. Grand Rapids: Eerdmans, 1987.

Holmes, Arthur F., ed., *The Making of a Christian Mind: A Christian
Worldview and the Academic Enterprise.* Downers Grove, Ill.: Inter-
Varsity Press, 1985.

Hunter, James Davison. *Culture Wars: The Struggle to Define America.*
New York: Basic Books, 1991.

Johnson, Luke Timothy. *Scripture and Discernment: Decision-Making in the Church.* Nashville: Abingdon, 1996.

Johnson, Phillip E. *Darwinism on Trial.* Downers Grove, Ill.: Inter-Varsity Press, 1993.

Jones, Peter. *Spirit Wars: Pagan Revival in Christian America.* Mukilteo, Wash.: WinePress, 1997.

Kraybill, Donald B. *The Puzzles of Amish Life.* Intercourse, Pa.: Good Books, 1990.

Kromminga, Carl G. "Christian Love and Offending the 'Weak': A Review Article." *Calvin Theological Journal* 28 (1993): 155–65.

Kuyper, Abraham. *Christianity as a Life System: The Witness of a Worldview.* Memphis: Christian Studies Center, 1980.

Lakeland, Paul. *Postmodernity: Christian Identity in a Fragmented Age.* Minneapolis: Fortress, 1997.

Latourette, Kenneth Scott. *A History of Christianity.* New York: Harper and Row, 1953.

Lewis, C. S. *Mere Christianity.* San Francisco: HarperSanFrancisco, 2001.

Lipset, Seymour Martin, ed. *The Third Century: America as a Post-Industrial Society.* Stanford: Hoover Institute Press, 1979.

Little, Bruce A. "Christian Education, Worldviews, and Postmodernity's Challenge." *Journal of the Evangelical Theological Society* 40, no. 3 (September 1997): 433–44.

Luther, Martin. "On Christian Liberty." In *Three Treatises.* Philadelphia: Muhlenberg Press, 1947.

Lyon, David. *Future Society: Life after 1984—Threat or Promise?* Belleville, Mich.: Lion, 1984.

———. *Postmodernity.* 2d ed. Minneapolis: University of Minnesota Press, 1999.

———. *The Steeple's Shadow.* London: SPCK, 1985.

Marsden, George M. *Fundamentalism and American Culture: The Shaping of Twentieth Century Evangelicalism.* New York: Oxford University Press, 1980.

Marsden, George M., ed. *Evangelicalism and Modern America*. Grand Rapids: Eerdmans, 1984.

Mayers, Marvin K. *Christianity Confronts Culture: A Strategy for Cross-Cultural Evangelism*. Grand Rapids: Zondervan, 1974.

Mayers, Ronald B. *Balanced Apologetics: Using Evidences and Presuppositions in Defense of the Faith*. Grand Rapids: Kregel, 1984.

McLaren, Brian D. *The Church on the Other Side: Doing Ministry in the Postmodern Matrix*. 1998. Reprint, Grand Rapids: Zondervan, 2000.

Meadows, Paul. *The Many Faces of Change: Explorations in the Theory of Social Change*. Cambridge, Mass.: Schenkman, 1971.

Meeter, H. Henry. *The Basic Ideas of Calvinism*. Grand Rapids: Baker, 1956.

Middleton, J. Richard, and Brian J. Walsh. *Truth Is Stranger Than It Used to Be: Biblical Faith in a Postmodern Age*. Downers Grove, Ill.: InterVarsity Press, 1995.

Moberg, David O. *The Church as a Social Institution*. 2d ed. Grand Rapids: Baker, 1984.

Monsma, Stephen, ed. *Responsible Technology*. Grand Rapids: Eerdmans, 1986.

Myers, Kenneth A. *All God's Children and Blue Suede Shoes: Christians and Popular Culture*. Wheaton, Ill.: Crossway, 1989.

Nash, Ronald H. *Christian Faith and Historical Understanding*. Grand Rapids: Zondervan, 1984.

Neuhaus, Richard John. *The Naked Public Square: Religion and Democracy in America*. Grand Rapids: Eerdmans, 1984.

Newbigin, Leslie. *Foolishness to the Greeks: The Gospel and Western Culture*. Grand Rapids: Eerdmans, 1986.

Nicholls, Bruce J. *Contextualizing: A Theology of Gospel and Culture*. Downers Grove, Ill.: InterVarsity Press, 1979.

Niebuhr, H. Richard. *Christ and Culture*. New York: Harper and Row, 1951.

Nisbet, Robert A. *History of the Idea of Progress*. New York: Basic Books, 1980.

————. *Social Change*. New York: Harper and Row, 1972.

Noll, Mark A. *The Scandal of the Evangelical Mind*. Downers Grove, Ill.: InterVarsity Press, 1994.

Nolt, Stephen N. *A History of the Amish*. Intercourse, Pa.: Good Books, 1992.

Packer, J. I. *Knowing God*. Downers Grove, Ill.: InterVarsity Press, 1993.

Plantinga, Cornelius, Jr. *Engaging God's World: A Christian Vision of Faith, Learning, and Living*. Grand Rapids: Eerdmans, 2002.

Pratt, Richard L., Jr. *Every Thought Captive: A Study Manual for the Defense of Christian Truth*. Phillipsburg, N.J.: Presbyterian and Reformed, 1979.

Rogers, Rex M. *Liberty: Christians Using Spiritual Discernment*. Grand Rapids: Cornerstone University, 2000.

———. *Seducing America: Is Gambling a Good Bet?* Grand Rapids: Baker, 1997.

Rookmaaker, H. R. *Modern Art and the Death of a Culture*. London: Inter-Varsity Press, 1970.

Rushdoony, Roussas. *The One and the Many: Studies in the Philosophy of Order and Ultimacy*. Fairfax, Va.: Thoburn Press, 1971.

Ryken, Leland. *Culture in Christian Perspective: A Door to Understanding and Enjoying the Arts*. Portland, Ore.: Multnomah, 1986.

Sayers, Dorothy L. *Christian Letters to a Post-Christian World: A Selection of Essays*. Grand Rapids: Eerdmans, 1969.

Schaeffer, Francis A. *Art and the Bible*. Downers Grove, Ill.: InterVarsity Press, 1973.

———. *A Christian Manifesto*. Westchester, Ill.: Crossway, 1981.

———. *The Church at the End of the Twentieth Century*. Downers Grove, Ill.: InterVarsity Press, 1970.

———. *Genesis in Space and Time: The Flow of Biblical History*. Downers Grove, Ill.: InterVarsity Press, 1972.

———. *The God Who Is There*. Downers Grove, Ill.: InterVarsity Press, 1968.

————. *The Great Evangelical Disaster.* Westchester, Ill.: Crossway, 1983.

————. *He Is There and He Is Not Silent.* Wheaton: Tyndale, 1972.

————. *How Shall We Then Live? The Rise and Decline of Western Thought and Culture.* Old Tappan, N.J.: Revell, 1976.

————. *The Mark of the Christian.* Downers Grove, Ill.: InterVarsity Press, 1970.

Schlossberg, Herbert. *Idols of Destruction: Christian Faith and Its Confrontation with American Society.* Washington, D.C.: Regnery Gateway, 1990.

Schultze, Quentin J., et al. *Dancing in the Dark:Youth, Popular Culture, and the Electronic Media.* Grand Rapids: Eerdmans, 1991.

Scott, Stephen. *Why Do They Dress That Way?* Intercourse, Pa.: Good Books, 1986.

Sine, Tom. *Wild Hope: Crises Facing the Human Community on the Threshold of the 21st Century.* Dallas: Word, 1991.

Sire, James W. *The Universe Next Door:A Basic Worldview Catalog.* 1976. Reprint, Downers Grove, Ill.: InterVarsity Press, 1988.

Smith, Anthony D. *The Concept of Social Change.* London: Routledge and Kegan Paul, 1973.

Smith, Gary Scott. *The Seeds of Secularization: Calvinism, Culture, and Pluralism.* Grand Rapids: Eerdmans, 1985.

Storkey, Alan. *A Christian Social Perspective.* Downers Grove, Ill.: InterVarsity Press, 1979.

Stott, John R. W. *Christian Counter-Culture:The Message of the Sermon on the Mount.* Downers Grove, Ill.: InterVarsity Press, 1978.

————. *Involvement: Being a Responsible Christian in a Non-Christian Society.* Old Tappan, N.J.: Revell, 1984.

Strauss, Richard L. *Win the Battle for Your Mind.* Neptune, N.J.: Loizeaux Brothers, 1986.

Taylor, Richard S. *A Return to Christian Culture.* Minneapolis: Dimension Books, 1973.

Tenney, Merrill C. *Galatians:The Charter of Christian Liberty.* Grand Rapids: Eerdmans, 1954.

Tidball, Derek. *The Social Context of the New Testament:A Sociological Analysis.* Grand Rapids: Zondervan, 1984.

Van Til, Henry R. *The Calvinistic Concept of Culture.* Grand Rapids: Baker, 1959.

Veith, Gene Edward, Jr. *Postmodern Times: A Christian Guide to Contemporary Thought and Culture.* Wheaton, Ill.: Crossway, 1994.

Vos, Howard F. *Galatians: A Call to Christian Liberty.* Chicago: Moody, 1971.

Walter, J. A. *Sacred Cows: Exploring Contemporary Idolatry.* Grand Rapids: Zondervan, 1979.

Watkins, William D. *The New Absolutes: How They Are Being Imposed on Us and How They Are Eroding Our Moral Landscape.* Minneapolis: Bethany, 1996.

Weber, Max. *The Protestant Work Ethic and the Spirit of Capitalism.* Translated by Talcott Parsons. New York: Charles Scribner's Sons, 1958.

Wecks, John. *Free to Disagree: Moving Beyond the Arguments over Christian Liberty.* Grand Rapids: Kregel, 1996.

Wiersbe, Warren. *God Isn't in a Hurry: Learning to Slow Down and Live.* Grand Rapids: Baker, 1994.

Wolfe, Alan. *Moral Freedom: The Impossible Idea That Defines the Way We Live Now.* New York: Norton, 2001.

Wolters, Albert M. *Creation Regained: Biblical Basis for a Reformational Worldview.* Grand Rapids: Eerdmans, 1985.

Rex M. Rogers earned degrees from Cedarville University and the University of Akron and holds a Ph.D. in political science and public administration from the University of Cincinnati. In 1991 Dr. Rogers was appointed president of Cornerstone University and its associated divisions Grand Rapids Baptist Seminary and CURadio. Since 1993 Dr. Rogers has produced a daily radio program called *Making a Difference,* applying a Christian worldview to contemporary social, political, economic, and religious issues.

Dr. Rogers's 1997 book *Seducing America: Is Gambling a Good Bet?* examined the economics and morality of the nation's infatuation with legalized commercial gambling. He has testified before the Michigan State Legislature as an expert witness on several occasions, spoken at many anti-casino rallies, and participated in more than 150 media interviews and programs on gambling, including *Focus on the Family,* Chris Fabry's *On Line,* and *Janet Parhsal's America.* Dr. Rogers's writings on economic issues have aired nationally on Larry Burkett's *Money Matters* and *Money Watch.*

Rex and his wife, Sarah, have four children and one grandchild.